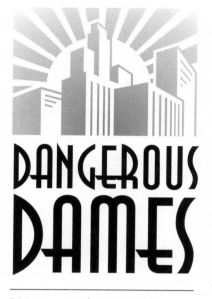

DANGEROUS DAMES

*Women and Representation
in the Weimar Street Film
and Film Noir*

JANS B. WAGER

OHIO UNIVERSITY PRESS • *Athens*

OHIO UNIVERSITY PRESS, ATHENS, OHIO 45701
© 1999 by Jans B. Wager
Printed in the United States of America
All rights reserved

Ohio University Press books are printed on acid-free paper ∞ ™

03 02 01 00 99   5 4 3 2 1

Library of Congress Cataloging-in-Publication Data

Wager, Jans B., 1958–
    Dangerous dames : women and representation in the Weimar
street film and film noir / Jans B. Wager.
        p.   cm.
    Includes bibliographical references and index.
    ISBN 0-8214-1270-1 (cloth : alk. paper)
    1. Femmes fatales in motion pictures. 2. Film noir—United
States—History and criticism. 3. Film noir—Germany—History and
criticism. 4. Street films—Germany—History and criticism. I. Title.
    PN1995.9F44 W35 1999
    769.92—dc21   98-49586
                                                            CIP

This book is dedicated
to my mother, Jane Wager,
always my assumed reader and
a superior editor.

CONTENTS

CONTENTS

PART FOUR: PASTS AND PRESENTS

ILLUSTRATIONS

ACKNOWLEDGMENTS

I would like to thank J. D. Davidson, Charles Vogel, and Utah Valley State College for support during the final stages of the publication process for this book, and Gail Finney and the Comparative Literature Program at the University of California, Davis, for support and encouragement throughout my graduate career. I thank Renate Möhrmann for her help acquiring texts and for her unbridled enthusiasm about my project, and Anna Kuhn for her help. Gudrun Weiss at the Friedrich Wilhelm Murnau Stiftung in Wiesbaden was gracious and generous and I thank her for facilitating my research. The Murnau Stiftung also provided kind permission for the use of images captured from *Asphalt*. Craig Gallichotte and Video Yesteryear provided kind permission for the use of images from *The Street* and *Variety*. Christina Frei and her family helped make my brief research time in Germany both productive and enjoyable.

I thank Tracy Wager for her impeccable graphic design sense and patient help with formatting images, Jane Wager for countless hours of editing, and Deidra Wager for financial support. My friend Leah Theis deserves thanks both for her companionship and for her editing and bibliographic help. Bill Nicholson's support imbues every page.

INTRODUCTION
Shot—Reverse Shot

Shot: Weimar street film

A restless man leaves his wife and their orderly middle-class home to seek excitement. He becomes entangled in the underworld, which seeks to implicate him in a murder. He returns home shaken and only too happy to stay in his safe environment thereafter.

> —Anthony Munson, description of first Weimar
> street film, *The Street*
> (*Die Straße*, Karl Grune, 1923)

Reverse shot: Weimar film

Close analysis of a wide spectrum of textual practices in Weimar . . . reveals that a female spectator was indeed assumed and addressed by such popular forms as the cinema and the illustrated press, and that these forms . . . refer to something other than male identity and male symbolic defeat.

> —Patrice Petro, *Joyless Streets*

Shot: film noir

[T]his fantasy is almost always a masculine scenario, that is, the film noir hero is a man struggling with other men, who suffers alienation and despair, and is lured by a fatal and deceptive woman.

> —Elizabeth Cowie, *"Film Noir* and Women"

Reverse shot: film noir

[T]he tendency to characterize film noir as always a masculine form . . . obscures the extent to which these films afforded women roles which are active, adventurous and driven by sexual desire.

> —Elizabeth Cowie, *"Film Noir* and Women"

I DO not deny that the Weimar street film often portrays a restless man seeking adventure outside the bounds of his middle-class existence, or that the film noir hero is often a man struggling with other men. But I agree with Patrice Petro and Elizabeth Cowie—both the Weimar street film and film noir tell other stories as well, stories that address a female spectator by providing her with various visual and narrative pleasures. I indulged in these pleasures as a film aficionada long before I became a film scholar. I used to scour the shelves of video stores searching for those luminous black-and-white films that I now identify as film noir. My growth as a feminist film scholar added a rich critical dimension to my viewing practices and an appreciation of film history beyond the confines of Hollywood. My task as film aficionada and feminist scholar is to account in part for my own fascination with film noir and the Weimar street film, cinematic texts that have historically been read as concerned primarily with male identity.

As early as 1947, in *From Caligari to Hitler*, Siegfried Kracauer articulates a teleological view of Weimar cinema in which, as Petro notes, "a sequence of historical events . . . is rewritten in terms of a . . . narrative of male passivity and symbolic defeat" (Petro 1989, 13). Although theorists such as Anton Kaes and Thomas Elsaesser refute elements of Kracauer's argument, for these critics the subject of Weimar cinema still remains masculine. In her 1996 essay "Woman as Sexual Criminal," Barbara Hales explores the fascinating connection between Weimar social discourses and the figure of the femme fatale. But Hales persists in reading the femme fatale solely as "a signifier for the fear of women's liberation" (Hales 1996, 12). Hales provides a portrait of a male subject and male fear, and elides the possibility of a female subjectivity. With a few notable exceptions, criticism of film noir has been similarly focused on male identity. Recent book titles, for example, include Frank Krutnik's *In a Lonely Street: Film Noir, Genre, Masculinity*, and James Maxfield's *The*

Fatal Woman: Sources of Male Anxiety in American Film Noir, 1941–1991.

For me, the thematic concerns that connect the Weimar street film, a product of Germany in the 1920s and early 1930s, with film noir, a product of Hollywood in the 1940s and 1950s, turn on the axis of female identity as well as male identity. I want to protect my personal investment in film noir and the Weimar street film by suggesting that the female audience, while certainly implicated in the patriarchal institution of cinema, also finds in cinema opportunities to resist dominant ideologies. Ben Agger conceives of "cultural studies in its best sense as an activity of critical theory that directly decodes the hegemonizing messages of the culture industry"[1] (Agger 1992, 5). I hope to decode some of the messages of the Weimar street film and film noir to provide a view concerned with female subjectivity—with the female spectator and the representation of women in film—derived in part from Patrice Petro's reading of Weimar cinema and E. Ann Kaplan's feminist criticism of film noir contained in *Women in Film Noir,* as well as Elizabeth Cowie's more recent essay "*Film Noir* and Women." Petro and Cowie concentrate on films that overtly address a female spectator; Petro discusses melodramatic films and Cowie, after somewhat redefining melodrama, focuses on films that feature a woman as the primary protagonist. I also discuss a melodramatic impulse that links Weimar street films to films noirs, but am more interested in texts that address a general (both male and female) audience, and in what these films might communicate to a female spectator. I agree with Agger that "[w]atchers are also potential cultural creators and historical subjects" (Agger 1992, 7). Both the Weimar street film and film noir doubtless explore a crisis in masculine identity. I will examine how these same films assume and address a female spectator, and attempt to help write the female subject into the critical history of the Weimar street film and film noir.

When I began this project in the early 1990s, film noir provided dark and stylistically intriguing texts for cinephiles and film theorists. Today Hollywood regularly produces retro-noirs such as *Mulholland Falls* (1995) and *L.A. Confidential* (1997) and neo-noirs such as *The Last Seduction* (1994) and *Twilight* (1998). The once mysterious style is ubiquitous in cinema, fashion, and the rest of popular culture. This study concludes with a discussion of recent noirs, both a German film and various Hollywood productions. I look again at appeals to the female spectator, as well as seek to account for the noir sensibility's persistence and increasing popularity.

PART ONE

Rethinking Paradigms

CHAPTER 1

Methodologies

Who's Seeing Whom: Representation and Identification

WHO, or what, is a female spectator? Barbara Creed delineates four constructs to which the notion applies: "the diegetic (the 'woman' on the screen); the imaginary (the construction of patriarchal ideology, the one to whom the film is addressed); the theorized (the creation of feminist criticism); and the real (the woman in the auditorium)" (Creed 1989, 133). My work necessarily deals more with the first three—the diegetic, the imaginary, and the theorized—than with the real, but not because I agree with Mary Ann Doane's assessment that "the female spectator is a concept, not a person" (Doane 1989, 143). Doane finds the issue of female spectatorship "already a historical concept" (142), one that has perhaps outlived its theoretical usefulness. But for me the divorce between the real woman in the audience and the concept of the female spectator is highly problematic. Just as she has been disavowed or ignored in feminist film criticism, she herself has ignored this criticism. Through the lenses of the diegetic, imaginary, and theoretical female spectator I approach, although never reach, the real. I approach the imaginary spectator through film criticism that focuses on male identity, and the theoretical spectator through my own readings of the diegetic woman on the screen. Although I can never know the real spectator who sat in the movie theater and watched the films I discuss, the real film aficionada remains my intended audience.

My intention is to communicate with a cinemagoer, male or

female, academic or nonacademic, feminist, antifeminist, or nonfeminist. This locates my work in the realm of the kind of cultural studies promoted by Agger, although I am unwilling to abandon traditional film studies completely. In *Star Gazing: Hollywood Cinema and Female Spectatorship*, Jackie Stacey contrasts film studies with cultural studies:

FILM STUDIES	CULTURAL STUDIES
Spectator positioning	Audience readings
Textual analysis	Ethnographic methods
Meaning as production-led	Meaning as consumption-led
Passive viewer	Active viewer
Unconscious	Conscious
Pessimistic	Optimistic
(Stacey 1994, 24)	

For Stacey, film studies proceeds from an institutional model of spectatorship that foregrounds the cinematographic apparatus, a concept central to the work of film theorist Jean Louis Baudry and many other theorists of the 1970s and 1980s. Robert Lapsley and Michael Westlake outline Baudry's view of the spectator as "blind to the work of the film," and "to the film's ideological operation" (Lapsley and Westlake 1988, 79). For Baudry, the result of the cinematographic apparatus is that "the spectator is constituted by the meanings of the text but believes him or herself to be their author" (80). My interest in film scholarship crosses back and forth between film studies and cultural studies, between acknowledging the operation of the cinematographic apparatus and denying its total hegemony. My own project utilizes both a film and a cultural studies approach to discuss representation and identification in film spectatorship.

Stacey engages in an ethnographic study of female filmgoers in Britain in the 1940s and 1950s. Stacey's attention to real women is both refreshing and informative, but her approach becomes difficult to apply to earlier cinemas. Distanced from the audience in the theater by the intervening years or by practical constraints, I must construct some image of the historical female spectator of Weimar cinema and of film noir. To do this I research production histories, reading reviews contemporary with the film's release in search of reviewers' attitudes toward technical innovations, toward the acting style, or toward gender. Since I am also interested in revising a critical history excessively concerned with male identity, I examine critical texts to see what they might say (or neglect to say) about female identity. The ways in which these critical texts delineate the diegetic women on the screen help me construct a version of the imaginary spectator positioned by the patriarchally determined cinematographic apparatus. I include this background in my analysis—details that aid in situating a film in its cultural context and help locate the female audience historically.

Textually, according to Stacey's view of film studies and the institutional model of spectatorship, the female spectator is always and forever positioned by the process of identification. Stacey pits the textual analysis of film studies against the ethnographic methods of cultural studies. While an ethnographic survey of the women and men who constituted the theater audience of films noirs and Weimar street films would be fascinating and informative, I cannot neglect close textual analysis. Through my own analysis of the diegetic women on the screen, I approach the theorized spectator—the creation, as Creed notes, of my own feminist criticism.

With whom does the spectator identify? As Judith Mayne suggests, Laura Mulvey's "visual pleasure" theory and other psychoanalytic theories are informed by the same assumptions, namely: "that identification in the cinema does proceed primarily in terms of individuals in the audience and characters projected on screen . . . and that identification is literal . . . so that men identify with male characters, women with female characters, and so on" (Mayne 1993, 26).[1] This type of identification does provide the most obvious position from which to theorize the imaginary spectator. The diegetic women and the cinematic text itself evoke the imaginary spectator but also provide a space into which I can insert my vision of a theorized spectator and propose a possible alternative to the dominant reading. Rarely does a Weimar street film or a film noir provide only one possibility for female identification. Part of my analysis includes exploring what options for same-sex identification the cinematic text provides the female spectator and how enticing those options appear. My construction of a theorized spectator rejects the notion of identification as a single position and assumes that cinematic identification is "a series of shifting positions . . . as fragile and unstable as identity itself" (Mayne 1993, 27).

This view of cinematic identification as a series of shifting positions is reiterated in the psychoanalytic reassessment of fantasy. Fantasy, by its nature, exists "for the subject across many possible positions" (Mayne 1993, 88). For Jean Laplanche and Jean-Bertrand Pontalis, fantasy "is not the object of desire but its setting" (Laplanche and Pontalis 1986, 26). Laplanche and Pontalis follow Freud, delineating three original fantasies, the primal scene, fantasies of castration, and fantasies of seduction (19). While these original fantasies reinscribe a psychoanalytic view of sexuality that I am not necessarily willing to perpetuate here, I find Laplanche and Pontalis's concept of fantasy useful for understanding how Weimar street films and films noirs might have provided the female spectator with certain pleasures. In fantasy, "the spectator engages in multiple identifications, and in its filmic scenarios may identify with several figures simultaneously, women and men, winners and losers, heroes and villains, the active and passive" (Lapsley and Westlake 1988, 92). As Mayne reiterates, the cinema is "a form of fantasy wherein the boundaries of biological sex or cultural gender, as well as sexual preference, are not fixed" (Mayne 1993, 88).

Stacey's conception of same-sex desire intersects with the discussion of fantasy as the "staging of desire . . . a form of mise en scène" (Mayne 1993, 88). Mayne suggests that "[f]ilm theory has been so bound up in heterosexual symmetry that . . . it ignored the possibility . . . that one of the distinct pleasures of the cinema may well be a 'safe zone' in which homosexual as well as heterosexual desires can be fantasized and acted out"

(97). Stacey argues against the rigid psychoanalytical dichotomy between desire, which involves wanting to have, and identification, which involves wanting to be, suggesting that both processes operate simultaneously. Drawing from the results of her survey of female moviegoers, Stacey discusses the spectator-star relationship as significantly concerned with "forms of intimacy between femininities" (Stacey 1994, 172). According to Stacey, "spectator/star relationships all concern the interplay between self and ideal. . . . The love of the ideal . . . may express a desire to become more like that ideal, but this does not exclude the homoerotic pleasures of love for that ideal" (174). In Weimar cinema and film noir, the femme fatale might provide a suitable vehicle for a conceptualization of identification that does not ignore same-sex erotic desire. As Stacey concludes, "it is precisely in same-sex relations that the distinction between desire and identification may blur most easily, and . . . therein lies their particular appeal" (176). The multiplicity of positions implied by this conception of identification complicates the discussion of spectatorship, but also enriches it and provides the basis for my discussion of identification.

Returning to Stacey's contrasting paradigm, I place the imaginary spectator and the construction of patriarchal ideology in the realm of film studies, which suggests that this spectator passively and unconsciously absorbs a production-led meaning. The theorized spectator posited by cultural studies is an active viewer who consciously devours a meaning, which the viewer's own consumption patterns have determined. Stacey's last contrasting pair suggests film studies is pessimistic while cultural studies is optimistic. I embrace Agger's and Stacey's conception of cultural studies as a means to circumvent the pessimism that I feel underlies much of psychoanalytic film criticism. Mayne notes, "[h]ow many times does one need to be told that individual film x, or film genre y, articulates the law of the father, assigns the spectator a position of male oedipal desire, marshals castration anxiety in the form of voyeurism or fetishism, before psychoanalysis begins to sound less like an

exploration of the unconscious and more like a master plot?"
(Mayne 1993, 68–69). I do not deny the existence of such a
master plot, but am more interested in other plots. The only
real spectator I can construct is one made, to a certain degree,
in my image; she is white, heterosexual, middle-class, and conscious of herself as a woman trying to negotiate her way
through a patriarchal society. She is both positioned by the
ideological apparatus of cinema and capable of recognizing
possibilities for resistance to dominant ideologies. She is both
the imaginary and the theorized spectator but always more
than that as well. I locate the imaginary spectator in part by de-
voting attention to those critics who view both the street film
and film noir as representations of unstable male identity. How
these theorists read the diegetic woman on the screen compared to how I read her becomes one avenue by which I approach the female spectator. Although much of what I say
about spectatorship also applies to the male spectator, I concentrate on the female spectator in order to begin to balance
the scales of scholarship on Weimar cinema and film noir,
which has been excessively concerned with male identity.

My view of cinema both as an institution that produces ideological positions for spectators and as a site of possible resistance to dominant ideologies is not as contradictory as it may
initially appear. Mulvey and others have suggested that part of
the pleasure cinema offers may be the staging of ideological
transgressions and their eventual recontainment. In my discussion of the Weimar street films and film noir I explore how emphatic or successful that eventual recontainment of ideological
transgression might seem for the female spectator. What makes
many of these texts particularly interesting for feminists is the
ambiguity that surfaces in narratives that have been historically
connected to unstable male identity.

Melodrama and Women

The Weimar Street Film and Film Noir as Crime Melodrama

ERTAIN thematic concerns connect the Weimar street film with film noir, and for me those concerns turn on the axis of female identity as well as male identity. Films produce meaning "through procedures and structures" that are historically and culturally specific, and "ideologically complicit" (Lapsley and Westlake 1988, 130). While I do not deny the ideological determinism that predicates much of film form, I am, to quote Laura Mulvey, especially interested in "the amount of dust the story raises along the way" (Mulvey 1989, 40).[1] Mulvey paraphrases Sirk, pointing out that the strength of the melodramatic form is the "cloud of overdetermined irreconcilables which put up a resistance to being neatly settled, in the last five minutes, into a happy end" (40). Both the Weimar street film and film noir offer instances that cannot be strictly contained within an ideological framework concerned exclusively with male identity, and both have been defined as melodramas.

The Film Encyclopedia defines German street films as "psychological melodramas in which the downtown street represented a dangerous lure and a force of tragic destiny for the imprudent male" (Katz 1994, 520). In *Joyless Streets: Women and Melodramatic Representation in Weimar Germany,* Patrice Petro explores the melodramatic impulse in numerous street films, focusing particularly on their appeal to a female spectator. Crime lurks and infects these melodramas through the contiguity of the street with the middle-class household. Films noirs have been similarly defined as crime melodramas. The term *film noir* came into common usage only after 1955, with the publication of Raymond Borde and Etienne Chaumeton's *Panorama du film noir américain*. Before then, as Elizabeth Cowie points out in *"Film Noir* and Women,"* many movies later called films noirs were identified in trade magazines such as *Variety* as crime melodramas or "mellers" (Cowie 1993, 129). Not surprisingly, like the Weimar street film, film noir's connection to melodrama is subsumed by the tendency to see every story as *his* story. As Cowie notes, most critics who make the connection between film noir and melodrama, "distinguish film noir as a form of male melodrama" (129).

Cowie, in contrast, identifies film noir as a kind of development in melodrama: "whereas the earlier obstacles to the heterosexual couple [in melodrama] had been external forces of the family and circumstances, wars or illness, in the film noir the obstacles derive from the characters' psychology or even pathology as they encounter external events" (Cowie 1993, 130). In the Weimar street film, the male character's psychology, or even pathology, also creates obstacles to a socially acceptable heterosexual coupling. Cowie's aim, like my own with the Weimar street film and film noir, is to challenge the characterization of film noir as always a male form. She accomplishes her task, in part, by listing a huge number of films noirs that provided women with strong roles. She also provides close analysis of various noirs with powerful female protagonists, including *Raw Deal* and *Secret beyond the Door* (both 1948). I agree with Cowie that in film noir the external forces of the family and circumstance have been internalized, but I also maintain that external traces of those forces remain in the diegetic world of film noir. The same is true of the Weimar street film. The home and family have a place in both types of film. In both, the crime and instability of the street and the dangerous allure of the femme fatale threaten to infect or destroy the middle-class home and family. Simultaneously, the home itself poses a problem or threat to the female spectator. Both types of film deal thematically with the stresses of urbanization and with women's increased presence in the public sphere. The psychology or pathology of both the male and female characters reflect those stresses. A type of melodramatic imagination charts a course from the Weimar street film to film noir.

Peter Brooks revitalizes the discussion of melodrama in *The Melodramatic Imagination* (1976). For Brooks, melodrama, as a form, "comes into existence near the start of the nineteenth century," with the French Revolution (Brooks, 1976, xi). With the toppling of such absolute and assumed values as God and King, the moral occult becomes the dramatic center of interest. According to Brooks, "The moral occult is not a metaphysical system; it is rather the repository of the fragmentary and de-sacralized remnants of sacred myth. It bears comparison to un-conscious mind, for it is a sphere of being where our most basic desires and interdictions lie, a realm which in quotidian exis-tence may appear closed off from us, but which we must accede to since it is the realm of meaning and value" (5). What inter-ests me in Brooks's evocative description of the moral occult is how it sums up the world of the crime melodrama in Weimar street films and film noir—a world that exists in the streets, be-yond the fringes of quotidian existence, a world that pulses with illicit desires and simultaneously acknowledges their nec-essary prohibition.

The renunciation necessary to rein in dangerous desire ac-quires special meaning in this desacralized system. Brooks as-serts, "The theme of renunciation is incomprehensible and un-justifiable except as a victory in the realm of a moral occult which may be so inward and personal that it appears restricted to the individual's consciousness, predicated on the individual's 'sacrifice to the ideal'" (5–6). God and King have been toppled, and their desacralized remains reside in the law and the man of the house. In the crime melodramas of the Weimar street film and film noir, the male characters seek to articulate the moral occult. In Weimar crime melodramas the erring husband or son discovers value in the domestic realm of the home and re-nounces the pleasures and dangers of the street. In film noir the detective or policeman usually operates according to his own

inner code of ethics, a code that inevitably requires that he re-
nounce what he most desires. But in both cycles of films, female
desire and female renunciation are also represented on the
screen.

Female characters in Weimar street films and film noir must
constantly renegotiate their positions in the desacralized cosmology of the moral occult, a cosmology that hints at subversive possibilities, at least from my late-twentieth-century feminist perspective. If the absolute patriarchy of God and King has
crumbled, might not the replacement patriarchy be equally or
more subject to siege? In Weimar crime melodrama, female
characters begin to awaken to the possibility of gaining power
for themselves. As we shall see, the Weimar street film portrays
the development of the wife from domestic somnambulist to
partner in marriage, and of the femme fatale from a prostitute
whose behavior is determined by her pimp to a woman acting
independently on her own desires and according to her own
inner code of ethics. In film noir the female characters continue
to push the boundaries of allowable feminine behavior, exerting pressure the women in the audience must have understood
and appreciated. As the female characters gain power and exert
agency, their sacrifices and renunciations become more noteworthy, and the forces aligned against them gain virulence.
The melodrama of the Weimar street film and film noir concerns both male and female characters and spectators. As in
other forms of melodrama, familial influences remain critical.

In the Weimar street film the family often appears on
screen, representing the antithesis to life on the streets, but to
assert that familial influences are crucial to film noir might seem
surprising. The archetypal array of characters in film noir are
not family members but rather the hard-boiled, trench-coated
detective; the beautiful, duplicitous, and greedy femme fatale
with a revolver shoved deep into the pocket of her fur coat; and
a fascinating complement of criminals ranging from sleazy and
violent hoodlums to their glib and urbane bosses. The film noir
narrative, with its aura of paranoia accentuated by nontradi-
tional lighting and mise en scène, usually plays out not in the

brightly lit kitchen or living room of a comfortable home but at night in dimly lit back streets glistening with rain or shadowy stairwells filled with looming shadows. But the familial realm that receives screen time in the Weimar street film still lurks in the recesses of film noir.

As Silvia Harvey notes in "Woman's Place: The Absent Family in Film Noir," "[o]ne of the recurrent themes in film noir is concerned with the loss of those satisfactions normally obtained through the possession of a wife and the presence of a family" (Harvey 1978, 27). Yet the institution of a family is itself ambiguous, for according to Harvey, the family in a film narrative serves as both the representation of repressive, hierarchical and patriarchal relations, as well as the only legitimate avenue for achieving sexual satisfaction, although "the expression of sexuality and the institution of marriage are at odds with one another" (30). For female characters, as well as spectators, familial institutions engender a special problematic. For Harvey, "[w]oman's place in the home determines her position in society, but also serves as a reflection of oppressive social relationships generally" (23). Like film noir, Weimar street films display ambivalence toward the family. While I do not claim Weimar street films and film noir are solely, or even primarily, concerned with representing women's experience, my project suggests a description of these films that takes into account women's experience. I propose that film noir, and Weimar street film before it, is concerned with the forced immobility of the woman placed in the role of wife, and with exploring options to that forced immobility outside and inside the family. The options, as Cowie notes, "afforded women roles which are active, adventurous and driven by sexual desire," and, I assert, must have provided the female spectator with certain visual and narrative satisfactions (Cowie 1993, 135).

Femmes Fatales and Femmes Attrapées

Female characters in film noir and the Weimar street film fall conveniently into two categories, the femme fatale and, according to Janey Place, "the woman as redeemer" (Place 1980, 50). Place sees the femme fatale as a combination of "aggressiveness and sensuality" and asserts that her visual movement "represents man's own sexuality, which must be repressed and controlled if it is not to destroy him" (46–47). In contrast, the woman as redeemer "offers the possibility of integration for the alienated, lost man into the stable world of secure values, roles and identities. She gives love, understanding (or at least forgiveness), asks very little in return . . . and is generally visually passive or static" (50). As Nicholas Christopher notes in *Somewhere in the Night: Film Noir and the American City*, the redeeming woman "is usually unrelievedly pallid and passive—to the point of repulsing us, as well as the hero" (Christopher 1997, 199). Place's essay discusses women in film noir and was first published in 1978, but these two archetypal characters work perfectly as the subject of most discussions of female representation in the Weimar street film as well as film noir.

The femme fatale remains one of the distinctive and alluring features in both types of film, and as I have mentioned, most discussions read the intriguing character of the femme fatale only relative to male fears about women. In *Femmes Fatales: Feminism, Film Theory and Psychoanalysis*, Mary Ann Doane notes that the "femme fatale emerges as a central figure in the nineteenth century," and remains one of the most "persistent incarnations" of modernity (Doane 1991, 1). Doane goes on to point out that it "is not surprising that the cinema, born under the mark of such a modernity as a technology of representation, should offer a hospitable home for the femme fatale" (2). Certainly, Weimar street films and films noirs owe much of their enduring ability to attract spectators to the appeal of the femme fatale. As Christopher notes, the femme fatale "is nearly always the more intriguing and energetic figure . . . imbued with intelligence, guile, charm, and unambiguous sexual electricity" (Christopher 1997, 197). But Doane and many others see this dangerous woman not as a possible site of female subjectivity but as a "symptom of male fears about feminism" (Doane 1991, 2).

Since my project involves rereading the Weimar street film and film noir in terms of women's experience and female characters, I want to retain but somewhat revise the useful delineation of women in film noir into these basic character types: the femme fatale and the woman as redeemer. The term *femme fatale* refers, of course, to the male victim of her wiles. The femme fatale might be a reflection of male fears, but she represents more than that. I will continue to use the term, but will redefine it to reflect my focus on the female characters. The femme fatale is dangerous and often deadly to male characters, but her actions almost always prove fatal to her as well. In both Weimar street film and film noir, if she escapes with her life she winds up metaphorically or actually imprisoned, her dangerous self-actualization contained. I continue to use the term *femme fatale*, but behind that descriptive appellation I see her own demise, which she orchestrates through her rebellion against ideologically acceptable female roles as clearly as she victimizes any male characters.[2] As for the nurturer, the woman as redeemer, I rename her *femme attrapée*, or woman trapped, and chart her acceptance of her position in the patriarchal family structure or her resistance to it. In both the Weimar street film and film noir, these archetypal characters play out remarkably similar roles. Both types of women are trapped by patriarchal authority—the femme fatale by her resistance, the femme attrapée by her acquiescence. Part of my goal is to rethink and redefine not only the subject of Weimar street film and film noir, but the representation of women in these films as well. To do that, I examine these representations through the lens of the female experience.

The ambiguity inherent in the role of the femme attrapée and in the familial realm, especially for women, might seem at odds with the fundamental manichaeism of the melodramatic imagination. But, as Brooks suggests, "melodrama is by no means finished, either as an outlook or as an aesthetic genre" (Brooks 1976, xiv). The moral occult, "the domain of operative spiritual values which is both indicated within and masked by the surface of reality," determines the form of the crime melodramas of Weimar street film and film noir (Brooks 1976, 5). In the street film, the operative spiritual values of good (in the home and embodied by the femme attrapée) and evil (on the street and embodied by the femme fatale) appear on the surface of the filmic reality, although ruptures appear even in the first street film. In film noir the operative spiritual values are often obscured by the dark shadows of ambiguity. Yet what drives the narratives of both the street film and film noir is a type of melodramatic impulse, however obscured by pools of murky light and pitch-black shadows. This impulse, "as a mode of conception and expression, as a certain fictional system for making sense of experience, as a semantic field of force," remains vibrant precisely because it changes with the times (xiii). My task, in part, is to chart those changes and explore their possible meanings for a female spectator.

PART TWO
Weimar Contexts and Texts

The Weimar Years
The Weimar Republic and Weimar Cinema

THE Weimar Republic, and with it Weimar cinema, is historically clearly circumscribed. On 9 November 1918, William
II, kaiser of Germany and king of Prussia, abdicated, clear-
ing the way for the proclamation of the first German democratic
government. Fifteen years later, in 1933, Hitler came to power,
emphatically ending both the Weimar Republic and the golden
age of German film. The Weimar Republic enjoyed a brief period of relative stability in the mid to late 1920s, and the films
I analyze are associated with this time, famous for its flourish-
ing artistic environment. In addition to cinematic artists, the
stable Weimar years nurtured and inspired visual artists, musi-
cians, poets, playwrights, novelists, philosophers, architects,
and scientists. But the Weimar years were primarily marked by
often violent economic and political turmoil. Developing along
with various artistic movements and political parties was the
German Worker's Party. Adolf Hitler joined the party, later
called the NSDAP, as its five hundred and fiftieth member (Johann and Junker 1970, 149). Beneath the surface stability of the
Weimar period, politicians struggled to keep the fledgling
democracy afloat, to reintegrate Germany into the European
community, to negotiate around an economically disastrous
war reparations program, and to maintain order as inflation
skyrocketed. Many Germans were ambivalent about the democratic experience their country had embarked upon.

In *Mothers in the Fatherland*, Claudia Koonz discusses this ambivalence both about democracy and women's suffrage, which were not the result of years of political activism but rather a by-product of Germany's defeat in World War I (Koonz 1987, 22). In Weimar Germany women for the first time enjoyed legal equality with men, but not economic or symbolic equality. A democratic constitution and the election of a government were implicit in the terms of the Treaty of Versailles. Thanks to the socialist influence, that constitution, as Richard McCormick notes in his essay on cinematic discourses in Weimar film, "offered German women the promise of legal equality for the first time in history" (McCormick 1993, 641).[1] Ironically, at the same time that women supposedly achieved equality under the law, the jobs they had been filling because of a shortage of (literally) manpower were being reappropriated by the six million men returning from the battlefields.[2] According to Koonz, the propaganda that encouraged women to enter the work force reversed direction, and even women's magazines promoted "[t]he man at the desk! The woman at the stove!!!" (Koonz 1987, 26–27). More than propaganda turned against working women. As Werner Thönnessen notes in *The Emancipation of Women*, legal decrees in 1919 and 1920 obliged employers to dismiss women according to the "following order of priority: 1. Women whose husbands had a job. 2. Single women and girls. 3. Women and girls who had only 1–2 people to look after. 4. All other women and girls" (Thönnessen 1973, 91). Whether they had held jobs or not, however, most women never left the housework behind. With these forces aligned against them it comes as no surprise that, as Petro points out, "the vast majority of women in Weimar . . . lived on unearned income, or pensions, or the earnings of children or husbands . . . in other words, did not work outside the home at all" (Petro 1989, 75).

Not all women retreated or were driven from the labor force that had wooed and won them during the war. For those of us reading history today, the iconography of the New Woman symbolizes those women who rejected the tradition of *Kinder, Küche, Kirche* (children, kitchen, church). Koonz describes the idealized New Woman as "youthful, educated, employed, socially free and autonomous" (Koonz 1987, 42). Petro relativizes this idealized portrait by pointing out that the job opportunities for women were primarily in the "least modern sectors of the economy: shops, bars, cafes, or the workshops . . . of male relatives" (Petro 1989, 75).

Women found themselves caught in double binds at every turn. While many women voted, and took part in government on the local and national level, new rights for women also introduced dissent and disunity. Women of the various political parties, classes, and ages pursued radically different agendas, often working at cross-purposes. Women were declared equal under new laws, which were still enforced by supporters of the old monarchy. They were forced to relinquish the freedoms and autonomy enjoyed during the war, and when they did choose or need to work outside the home, the work often did not replace housework but rather added a menial form of employment to an already exhausting schedule. Yet McCormick, Koonz, and Petro all insist that the New Woman existed; she was not just a symbolic figure in the cultural discourse of Weimar Germany. Renate Bridenthal, Atina Grossman, and Marion Kaplan agree: "[t]he 'new woman'—who voted, used contraception, obtained illegal abortions, and earned wages . . . existed in office and factory, bedroom and kitchen" (Bridenthal et al. 1984, 11). And her presence, according to Petro, "in places [she] had never been before (notably, in industry and in the cinema) explains the perceived threat of woman registered in various discourses during the Weimar years" (Petro 1989, 71).

The New Woman's presence exacerbated a masculine crisis of identity stemming from defeat on the battlefields and perceived submission at the peace negotiation tables. The "stab in the back" legend gained popularity, attributing defeat in the war to subversive forces on the home front: Jews, Communists, Social Democrats, and, as Bridenthal, Grossman, and Kaplan point out, women (Bridenthal et al. 1984, 7). In Weimar Germany the perceived threat of the New Woman, of female

presence and power outside the realm of the home, was miti-
gated by the conservative cult of motherhood, which the Nazis
would later institutionalize. In Nazi Germany, "Mother's Day
was changed to Hitler's mother's birthday and made into a national holiday" (Koonz 1987, 186). As Koonz makes clear, the
Nazis reinforced the material and psychological incentives en-
couraging motherhood with "coercive policies" (186). Physically and racially fit women were obligated to have as many
children as possible, supposedly ensuring the propagation of
the Germanic bloodline while simultaneously keeping women
in their traditional roles. True to form, the Nazis eradicated the
threat of the New Woman and made motherhood a matter of
public policy. But before the Nazis came to power, the crisis in
masculine identity occupied the cultural imagination of
Weimar Germany.

Female identity remained invisible, while the male identity
crisis takes its place center stage in film criticism as early as
1947 in Siegfried Kracauer's *From Caligari to Hitler.* Making the
male spectator the historical subject of Weimar film, Kracauer
discusses his passivity and symbolic defeat in an endless round
of oedipal narratives leading inevitably to complete submission
to Hitler. Yet female identity also underwent an acute and radical crisis in Weimar Germany. I center my discussion on the female spectator as historical subject, without denying the presence of the male spectator in the audience or the male crisis in
identity reflected in these cultural discourses. Like Petro, I insist
that women were in the audiences as well and that they in some
way saw their own experiences represented on the screen.

Weimar cinema screens contained many images that inform
the ideological and artistic underpinnings of the Weimar street
film and later, of film noir. In the early years of the Weimar Republic, screens were filled with the sumptuous and extremely
popular historical costume dramas of Ernst Lubitsch and expressionist films such as *The Cabinet of Dr. Caligari (Das Cabinett des
Dr. Caligari,* 1919/20), and *Nosferatu* (1921/22). *Caligari,* directed
by Robert Weine, tells the story of the evil Dr. Caligari and his
somnambulist vassal, who acts out Caligari's murderous desires.

This film functioned as an expressionistic set piece, using production design to render the internal and subjective visible. With sets painted by three expressionist artists, the film is a series of arranged scenes shot by a usually immobile camera as figures move across its field of vision. As David Cook remarks in *A History of Narrative Film*, "Caligari imported Expressionism into the cinema but did not exploit it in cinematic terms . . . as a narrative structure" (Cook 1981, 115). In the vampire film *Nosferatu*, directed by F. W. Murnau, expressionism becomes cinematic. This film's deep-focus photography, low-angle camera work, unsettling editing, and chiaroscuro lighting effects usher in a visual style that will later become the stock-in-trade of the street film and, as McCormick notes, film noir.

McCormick subtitles his essay on Weimar film "From Caligari to Dietrich" and traces a shift in the cinematic depiction of male fears about women that begins with vampires or feminized monsters, Nosferatu and Cesare respectively, to a phallic or powerful woman such as Lola Lola by the end of the film *The Blue Angel (Der blaue Engel*, 1930) and explains how the image of the monstrous other becomes one with the image of the threatening woman (McCormick 1993, 648–49). McCormick traces a continuum from Nosferatu to the feminized foreign seducer Artinelli in *Variety* (1925), a film I will return to in more detail later, to the robot Maria in *Metropolis* (1925/26). This continuum ends with *The Blue Angel* and the transformation of Lola Lola from a theatrical phenomenon on a stage in front of an audience, to "cinematic" illusion; she sits alone on a empty stage and the spectator has become the audience. McCormick does not ignore the presence of women as spectators or deny Weimar film's depiction of male fantasies. He seeks to "demonstrate the social and political dimensions of these fantasies as well as the stakes their deployment posed for women" (642).

My project is similar to McCormick's, but I focus my analyses differently. While trying to avoid the reactive position that these ideologically patriarchal texts can be reappropriated and reread in a subversive way, I want to suggest that not only male fantasies but also female fantasies appeared on the screens. I plan to engage in a dialogue with criticisms focused on male identity and, through a close textual reading of certain films, to suggest ways in which the female spectator and female identity were addressed. McCormick points out that the feminine ideal of the seductive vamp "works ultimately in the service of consumer capitalism: it implies that to become a desirable commodity is powerful" (664). Again, I do not disagree with McCormick but hope to show that the vamp may be read as more than a commodity showcase. I will also suggest that the continuum traced by McCormick from monster to vamp suggests other directions that must be explored in order to take into account female identity.

In *Joyless Streets: Women and Melodramatic Representation in Weimar Germany*, Patrice Petro manages to resist the seductive image of the vamp as a sole focus and concentrates instead on Weimar melodramatic films. Petro's study, which includes an analysis of the illustrated press and cinema of the period, begins with a discussion of Weimar theories of mass culture and modernism. Weimar intellectuals associated mass culture with the supposedly feminine characteristics of "passivity, vulnerability, [and] even corruption," while modernism demanded a "masculine" activity, distance, and intellectual engagement (Petro 1989, 8). Such a constellation reinforces the stereotype of female passivity at the same time as it bolsters the illusion of male superiority and mastery. It also precludes the possibility of active female subjectivity and, as Petro points out, "reemerges in contemporary histories of Weimar cinema" (9). Petro examines Kracauer's view of Weimar cinema as a mass cultural phenomenon and discusses critic Thomas Elsaesser, who in a series of essays in 1980 defined Weimar film as modernist—a "self-conscious art cinema" (15). Yet for both theorists, "whether the object of Weimar cinema . . . is mass cultural or modernist, the subject remains the same—" male (17). In order to shift the substance of the debate, Petro concentrates on cultural forms that made an address specifically to women, whether in the illustrated press or, more consequential for my purposes, in street films.

The films I focus on in this study represent a selection of texts from an extensive Weimar filmography, a selection that begins in 1923, as the influence of the expressionist *Schauerfilme* (horror films) and historical *Kostümfilme* (costume films) waned in favor of new objectivity and a certain realism best represented by the street film. I focus on films made primarily by the notoriously conservative UFA (Universum Film, A.G.), and I avoid the output of the German left, such as Prometheus production company's *Mother Krause's Journey to Happiness* (*Mutter Krausens Fahrt ins Glück*, 1929), and semidocumentary slice-of-life films such as *Berlin, Symphony of a Great City* (*Berlin, Die Sinfonie der Großstadt*, 1928).[3] In *Joyless Streets*, Petro concentrates her analyses on melodramatic films that specifically address a female audience. Petro mentions *The Cabinet of Dr. Caligari*, *Nosferatu*, *Metropolis*, and a number of other movies but concentrates on the street films of Henny Porten and Asta Nielson, specifically *Backstairs* (*Hintertreppe*, 1921), *The Joyless Street* (*Die freudlose Gasse*, 1925), *Tragedy of the Whore* (*Dirnentragödie*, 1927), and *Refuge* (*Zuflucht*, 1928). In each of her discussions Petro pays explicit attention to female subjectivity. She discusses a recurring image in Weimar street films, that of "a female figure [who] stands outside a locked or closed door and begins knocking, then pounding, as if to express the force of an ineffable desire and anger" (Petro 1989, 218). For Petro, this image makes its appeal directly to the female spectator, speaking of the "promises and failures of sexual and economic liberation in Weimar" (218). It also provides a female equivalent to an image Kracauer identifies as "a singular gesture of capitulation" that often appears in Weimar cinema, that of a man who breaks down, "and while his mother caresses him as if he were a child, he rests his head helplessly on her bosom" (Kracauer 1947, 99). The texts I discuss are also street films, but not ones directed specifically at a female audience. Petro's study constructs a female spectator interested in consuming images that address her understanding of and problems with traditional gender roles. I will elaborate on Petro's work by suggesting that even those films not designed to appeal to a specifically female audience address similar problems and were understood by the women in the audience to reflect, to some degree, their experiences. These films cannot be labeled subversive. Like Hollywood cinema and film noir, they were intended to appeal to a mass audience as entertainment and if they supported any political agenda it was, as Thomas Plummer and others point out in *Film and Politics in the Weimar Republic,* an ideologically conservative one.

I will suggest a continuity between the Weimar street film and film noir that hinges on the increased activity of female characters and on the problematic relationship between the realm of the street and the realm of the family. As I mention earlier, like many films noirs, the Weimar street films might also be labeled crime melodramas—in both cycles of films, the crime and instability of the street threatens to infect or destroy the middle-class home and family. At the same time, the portrayal of the domestic realm is itself ambiguous. The Weimar street film, according to Bruce Murray in *Film and the German Left in the Weimar Republic,* "affirmed patriarchal concepts of the family and sexuality" (Murray 1990, 81). Although these films often portrayed middle-class domestic security as stiflingly monotonous, the streets, Murray notes, were "inherently dangerous, evil places, dominated by prostitutes, pimps, criminals, and alcoholics" (82). While I do not intend to ignore male characters in my discussion of Weimar street films or films noirs, my focus will be on the representations of women and how those representations change from the first street film, *The Street (Die Straße,* 1923), to the late street film *Asphalt* (1929), and then from the first film noir, *The Maltese Falcon* (1941), to the late film noir *The Big Heat* (1953). I will take note of those instances that seem to be specifically directed toward a female spectator and might reflect her experiences or desires.

The Street Rules
The Weimar Street Film
and *The Street*

> The street rules, the street shines, the street begins
> to speak. She is the main character.
>
> (Die Straße regiert, die Straße leuchtet, die Straße
> hebt zu sprechen an. Sie ist die Hauptdarstellerin.)
>
> —Opening title, *The Street* (*Die Straße*, 1923)

I N the first Weimar street film, the street itself provides the locus for dangers and enticements, which will be embodied by the femme fatale in later Weimar films, and in film noir. But the home and family have a place in both types of film as well. In both, the crime and instability of the street and the dangerous allure of the femme fatale threaten to infect or destroy the middle-class home and family. At the same time, as noted earlier, the home itself poses a problem or threat to the female spectator. Patrice Petro notes the pervasive use in 1920s German scholarship and journalism of "the figure of woman as metaphor for the enigmatic, and hence, desirable 'otherness' of the city" (Petro 1989, 40). In the street films of Weimar cinema the desirable "otherness" and potential destructiveness of the urban milieu are increasingly expressed in the figure of the femme fatale. Conversely, undesirable sameness and dull safety reside not in rural environs but in the domestic sphere of the family, usually presided over by a wife or mother.

Directed by Karl Grune and produced by Stern-Film, *The Street* (*Die Straße*, 1923) is generally considered to be the first

Weimar street film, and the film's plot provides the paradigm for many street films to follow: a male protagonist is lured from his solid, middle-class existence into the seductive world of the street. Once he experiences the dangers and disappointments of the street, he returns gratefully home, ready to dutifully resume his former life. Many films noirs, including *The Woman in the Window* (1945), directed by Fritz Lang, provide updated versions of this paradigm. Although I am interested in tracing a continuum that focuses on the representation of women and the transformations these representations undergo, the large number of directors and film technicians who abandoned or fled Germany for Hollywood also provide continuity between the Weimar cinema and film noir. My focus will be primarily on the representations of women, but I will also explore those representations of diegetic "men" I read as appealing specifically to a female spectator. *The Street* does include a prototypical femme fatale, a prostitute. Visually and narratively, however, the danger and allure that will settle on the figure of the femme fatale in later crime melodramas are located in the urban streets themselves, in the pools of light cast by the streetlamps on dark city streets and in the sidewalk cafés and nightclubs. As Barbara Hales notes in her discussion of the criminal femme fatale and the street film, the "street itself seems to play the role of the prostitute, as the protagonist falls under its spell" (Hales 1996, 110). Despite the shift of narrative and visual attention to the femme fatale, later Weimar street films retain a fascination with the streets, and dark, rain-soaked city streets become an almost obligatory visual trope of film noir.

The Weimar street film followed on the heels of Germany's expressionistic *Schauerfilme*, and *The Street* does not completely abandon those roots; it transports expressionistic lighting, photography, and symbolism into a realistic narrative. In the film, as Lotte Eisner describes in *The Haunted Screen*, the street enters directly into the action: "as a luminous temptation from a middle class dining room, an invitation cast through the window by the lurid life outside, in the form of light wavering in the gloom and printing a furtive lace-pattern on the ceiling, provoking longings in . . . the meticulous bourgeois" (Eisner 1969, 252). This luminous temptation takes the form of a shadow play on the wall and ceiling of a darkened parlor, as the soon-to-be "rebellious philistine," as Kracauer calls him, lazes on the sofa, waiting for his dinner to be served. He looks up and sees the figure of a woman emerging from the rushing shadows of the street. She is approached by a man wearing a bowler hat and carrying an umbrella, who greets her and follows her into the flux of shadows. For Anton Kaes in *Geschichte des deutschen Films,* this scene makes a cinematic reference: "the magic of the street becomes identified with the magic of the cinema itself: in the very first scene the man observes on the wall a light-and-shadow play of pulsating life, as in a film projection."[1] But shadow play also becomes a layered homology for the movie when examined in terms of male identification and fantasy. The bored husband in the parlor becomes the male spectator in the cinema; both identify with the male protagonist of the shadow play, and each sees an image of a woman as the object of his desire.

The man on the screen accepts the street's invitation and rushes from the comfortable family parlor just as the soup is served by his dutiful wife. He attracts the attention of a prostitute, who easily lures him into a series of adventures, which end in the murder of another man by her business associates. The philistine is framed for the crime and, now subdued by the terrors of the street, feels too guilty even to profess his innocence. He almost commits suicide in jail before he is cleared of the crime. For Kracauer, *The Street* and many other Weimar films represent this development from rebellion to submission. When the one-time rebel returns home, dragging himself with resignation up the stairs to the rewarmed soup and the equally resigned embrace of his wife, Kracauer sees an "instinctive reluctance to attempt emancipation that might be considered a typical German attitude" (Kracauer 1947, 99). Kracauer's inability to see anything but the repetition of this pattern in Weimar film history should not surprise us. Those familiar with psychoanalytic film criticism know of the endless round of oedipal rivalries and unsuccessful challenges to patriarchal authority that is said to determine all of film form. Other arts naturally illustrate the same predilection. For example, father-son rivalries and tensions pervade much of Weimar painting and literature.

There is nothing emancipatory in the portrayal of the women in *The Street*. In the opening sequence of the film, the wife performs her domestic tasks with such ponderous inevitability that she becomes part of the stifling mise en scène against which the husband, and the audience, if it hopes for entertainment, must rebel. Yet she does function as an eternally loving anchor for her husband. The first shot of the wife in the film is masked—an opaque screen blocks off part of the frame. The most common mask is a round iris, which can close down or open out for emphasis. But the opening mask for the wife is heart-shaped, and shows her working at the stove in the well-lit kitchen.[2] As the mask fades, she briefly pats her hair into place and takes a tray of dishes into the parlor. Another series of shots in the opening sequence emphasizes the difference between the husband and wife, further aligning the wife with the dutiful acceptance of everyday life and the husband with dreams of a more exciting existence. The sequence makes the film's focus on the male protagonist explicit, while simultaneously locating desire and death in the figure of a woman.

The husband gets up from the sofa and is drawn to the window, apparently hoping to see some evidence of the seductive scene he saw acted out as a shadow play on the ceiling of the parlor. As he stands gazing out the window, the iris that shows his view of the street fades into an expressionistic vision of superimposed images: a clown's face, circus rides, fireworks, smoke, couples dancing, a woman smiling invitingly, a man with an accordion and parrot. But the final image in the kaleidoscope of enticements is the figure of a women, her face a death mask.[3] The street offers the man amusement, excitement, sexual adventure—all things his bourgeois home definitively lacks. But it also threatens danger, and even death, in the form of a woman. Again, this common dichotomy of both danger and allure embodied by a female figure is far from exclusive to film.

Meanwhile, the other diegetic woman, the wife, apparently wondering what her husband gazes at so longingly (if not why he looks back to her with an expression of disgust), goes to the window as well. She sees no vision of tempting wonders but simply the view from the parlor window—a busy street, bustling with automobiles, bicycles, pedestrians, and dust. She returns to the table and serves the soup. As she sits to eat, her husband, with a fearful glance at wife and table, rushes out the door. At dawn (and at the end of the film) as her errant husband returns home after a night of attempted debauchery, the wife sleeps, head in arms, at the dining table (fig. 1). This cinematic tableau, which "arrests narrative development so as to offer fixed representation," seems to suggest that the wife's sense of order and stability does not allow her to proceed past the

Figure 1. The narrative and visual immobility of the wife (*The Street,* 1923)

interrupted supper (Petro 1989, 32). Just as the shadow play described earlier serves as a homology for male identification, female identification can be aligned with the wife's vision. While the cinema offers the male spectator specific pleasures associated with heterosexual eroticism, the female spectator, if she engages only in same-sex identification, is denied a similar fantasy. As I mentioned earlier, if the female spectator seeks vicarious adventure, she must tag along with the male protagonist. Husband and wife both look out the same window, but she cannot see what he sees, and the narrative of *The Street* follows his vision.

The sequence described above, which shows the wife looking out the window, and the husband leaving the wife and soup behind, presents a total of nine shots in one minute and forty seconds. *The Street* displays a technical virtuosity that belies its immobile camera, creating the illusion of movement by the use of differing camera distances in each shot, and by the variety of techniques used to transition from one shot to another. A shot sheet helps map the sequence.

1. Close-up (head) of man at window.
Cut
2. To medium shot of woman at the table.
Cut
3. To medium shot of man at window; wife joins him in frame.
Cut
4. To close-up of wife looking, point-of-view shot.
Fade-out to black. Fade-in
5. To a long shot of the street, bustling with people and traffic.
Fade-out to black.
Fade-in
6. To close-up of wife looking; her eyes widen and then narrow. She turns from the window.
Superimposition
7. Of medium-long shot of wife walking back to table.
Cut

8. To medium shot of husband still at window, looking out of frame toward wife and table, with disgust.
Cut
9. To medium-long shot of both of them, separated by distance of room. They move toward each other; she sits to eat; he rushes from the room. She turns and looks at the door.

A close reading allows us to admire the technical sophistication of the 1923 film, and to see how the visual information provided in *The Street* allows the wife to move only within the prescribed perimeters of kitchen and parlor, while the husband's imagination and actual movements allow him to burst from the domesticity that contains her.

This vision of stupefying domesticity serves as the dominant representation of family life in *The Street*. Yet almost immediately after the rebellious philistine rejects another dinner with his wife and escapes to the early evening of the street, another family is introduced in which the woman seems completely absent. An iris opens on an old, apparently blind man sitting in a chair, caressing the hair of a small child who stands next to him, his arm on the old man's leg.[4] A young man enters the room, picks up his hat and prepares to go out, although the youngster begs him, "Don't leave me, Daddy."[5] He leaves, causing the child to burst into tears. The young man turns out to be the pimp of the prostitute in the narrative. The pimp will later be at least partially responsible for the murder of another man, and he attempts to get that murder pinned on the film's protagonist. In a tale that presents a dichotomy between the security of middle-class monotony and the overwhelming dangers of the lower-class life of the street, the innocence of a child and helplessness of the blind man provide a counterpoint to the supposed evils of their milieu.

With her focus on the woman as sexual criminal, Barbara Hales reads *The Street* differently. Hales asserts the prostitute is the mother of the child. The child does identify the pimp as its father in the scene I discuss above but never calls the prostitute

Mother. The only time the woman and the child share the screen, in the police station after the protagonist's adventures, the woman wraps the child in her cloak. For Hales, this brief interlude implies that "the daughter [of the prostitute] may in time follow the lead of her mother (and her criminal father)" (Hales 1996, 112). No textual evidence substantiates Hales's reading of the prostitute as mother of the child, and no unambiguous evidence suggests the gender of the child is female. Identified only as Sasha, the child actor was probably a boy. Mordaunt Hall, film reviewer for the *New York Times*, also sees the child as a boy, noting that "a little child in a nightgown . . . reveals that his father [the pimp] is lying [about his whereabouts at the time of the murder]" (M. Hall 1927, 34:3).

While I read the prostitute in *The Street* as a prototypical femme fatale, capable of acting only at the beck and call of her pimp, Hales sees her as a "trickster and an exhibitionist," who "uncovers her true inclinations by seducing the film's protagonist in her rundown apartment" (Hales 1996, 109, 111). I am not denying the prostitute's role in seducing the middle-class protagonist, but Hales neglects to mention that the pimp goads the woman into it. After leaving the child and old man, the pimp seeks her out at a sidewalk café and tells her, "We're broke; you've got to find some greenhorns," setting the seduction in motion. The pimp lurks in the background, motivating the prostitute's every action. Hales focuses on the cultural currency of the Weimar period, which insisted that "woman drives man to commit illegal deeds" (111), and finds proof of that assertion in *The Street*. I suggest another reading of the film, which admits the criminality of the woman but sees the impetus for that criminality in the pimp.

The Street, according to its own subtitle, tells "die Geschichte einer Nacht" (the story of a night).[6] It does tell the tale of a man who attempts to dabble in the world outside his parlor window and proves to be ill equipped to handle the excitement, danger, and duplicity of the urban milieu; but *The Street* does not elide another story. At the end of the film, as the rebellious philistine submits, two people of the street, disadvantaged by age and infirmity if not class, are left without a protector or provider. While the middle-class man returns to his safe and monotonous domesticity, the life of the lower-class family presented in the film has been radically altered, their tenuous if tender relationships severely threatened, their future uncertain. A number of Weimar street films follow *The Street*'s model, not only by telling the tale of male symbolic defeat or submission, but by allowing the middle-class characters to escape the street and return to or maintain their bourgeois existences while the lower-class individuals sink into despair or death. As Petro makes clear in *The Joyless Streets*, even films such as *Tragedy of the Whore* (*Dirnentragödie*, 1927) and *The Joyless Street* (*Die freudlose Gasse*, 1925), which make gender a central concern, do not ignore issues of class. Significantly, issues of class will become less and less notable as Weimar cinema matures, while issues of gender remain crucial.

The lack of spaces for same-sex female identification in the first street film seems remarkable. In my reading of *The Street*, the prostitute takes a role in moving the narrative forward, but she clearly operates at the beck and call of her pimp, and the motivation for her actions do not go much beyond his requirements. The wife of the rebellious philistine serves as a millstone around his neck, anchoring him firmly in his humdrum existence. She remains trapped in the parlor her husband can escape, completely immobilized by the narrative. Women in the audience are not specifically addressed or invited into the world of the film. *The Street*'s technical virtuosity would thrill all viewers, and the morality tale would be available to imaginary spectators of either gender.[7] But beginning with *The Street*, the realm of the private comes face to face with the realm of the public street and in both realms the figure of a woman remains central.

Female Desire

The Varigated Nature of
Desire in *Variety*

HE street film *Variety* (1925) also contrasts the domestic
with the public realm, and hints at possible subversions of
gender roles. For Kracauer, *Variety* again emphasizes the
motif found in many Weimar films—"the leading character
breaks away from the social conventions to grasp life, but the
conventions prove stronger than the rebel and force him into
either submission or suicide" (Kracauer 1947, 123). This motif
certainly provides a thumbnail sketch of *Variety*. In the film, a
prisoner tells his story to a benevolent judge. Once a trapeze
performer in a small-time circus, he left his faded blonde wife
and his child for an exotic dark-haired dancer, only to be betrayed by her and driven to the murder of her lover. Despite his
bulk, Emil Jannings plays the trapeze artist "Boss" Huller sincerely, and the camera work convincingly hides the substitu-
tions that must have been made during the circus performances. The scenes that describe the excessive monotony of
Huller's married life are contrasted explicitly with the sensuous
pleasures offered by Berta Maria (Lya de Putti), the exotic
dancer, and inscribe a domestic prison that parallels the drawing room of the rebellious philistine in *The Street*. Like *The Street*,
Variety tells the story of a man who escapes a stupefying family
life and elides the story of the femme attrapée, the wife who
cannot leave. Despite the predictability of the motif described
above, *Variety* also defies certain gender expectations, and the

film occasionally takes the ambiguous nature of visual pleasure and desire as its explicit topic.

The female characters in *Variety* repeat the femme attrapée/femme fatale dichotomy. As I have suggested, the wife in *Variety* is portrayed much like her counterpart in *The Street*. As I described earlier, the wife in *The Street* seems unable to move beyond the narrow confines of her domestic tasks. Her immobility renders her almost invisible, both visually and narratively, except as part of the dull and stable world to which the once rebellious man will return. In *Variety*, once Boss Huller abandons her and their child, the wife appears only as a story element in the final reel of the film. A title card reveals the contents of a letter written by the faithful wife to her jailed husband:

> I implore heaven that my request will be heard, that
> you will return to your child again. Your child knows
> nothing of this, and everyday watches for his father,
> whom he believes is far away in a foreign land . . . [1]

Her letter disavows any personal desires in favor of the child's needs, and her nonpresence on the screen further relegates the wife to cinematic obscurity.

Although she is discussing Hollywood film, Silvia Harvey describes the ideological position of the femme attrapée in both *Variety* and *The Street*: "The family . . . has served a crucial function in inserting within the film narrative the established values of competitive, repressive and hierarchical relationships. The presence of the family has served to legitimate and naturalize these values: that is, to present them as the normal, natural and unthought premises for conducting one's life. . . . Woman's place in the home determines her position in society, but also serves as a reflection of oppressive social relationships generally" (Harvey 1978, 23). Certainly the visual and narrative immobility of the wives epitomizes the oppressive social relationships that Harvey evokes. I suspect that in order to appeal to women, who were in the majority in film audiences in

Weimar Germany, Weimar cinema had to offer the female spectator some other versions of femininity, whether socially acceptable or not.

Unlike the passive femme attrapée, the femme fatale demands the attention of the camera and the spectator, as Berta Maria often does in *Variety*. Place, discussing the femme fatale in film noir, describes her visual importance: "The strength of these women is expressed in the visual style by their dominance in composition, angle, camera movement and lighting. They are overwhelmingly the compositional focus, generally centre frame and/or in the foreground, or pulling focus to them in the background. They control camera movement, seeming to direct the camera (and the hero's gaze, with our own) irresistibly with them as they move" (Place 1980, 45). Eisner's description of Berta Maria's initial appearance on the screen in *Variety* provides a specific filmic example of the visual dominance of the femme fatale. According to Eisner, "climbing the caravan steps Lya de Putti is seen as a forehead and a pair of immense eyes, then slowly, like a sunrise, her entire face appears, and the mundane fairground seems to be transformed into a metaphysical parable" (Eisner 1969, 281). Berta Maria does not exert this transformative power in every sequence, but her body and face provide innumerable instances for objectification.

Berta Maria does enjoy more agency than the prostitute in *The Street*. She actively pursues Boss Huller and willingly cuckolds him when she takes another lover. For Place, the difference between the "dangerous lady of film noir" and the "vamp seductress of the twenties" is "ambition expressed metaphorically in her freedom of movement and visual dominance" (Place 1980, 46). I suggest that the femme fatale, even in these early Weimar films, has a great deal in common with her counterpart in film noir, both in her ambition and her visual presence. The film noir woman's desire for "freedom, wealth or independence" does outstrip Berta Maria's attempts to increase her social standing within the circus milieu (46). Boss Huller raises her from abandoned dancing girl to acrobat with a provincial circus. Artinelli, his previous partner (and brother) injured in a fall, hires Huller as catcher and Berta Maria as trapeze artist for a spectacular variety show in the Berlin Wintergarten. With the famous and distinguished artist Artinelli (Warwick Ward), Berta Maria becomes a star performer.

For Mordaunt Hall, "Artinelli's surrender to the attractive girl is gradual and natural" (M. Hall 1926, 15:5). Hall's understanding of Berta Maria ignores certain visual and verbal information that enables a different reading. Let me reiterate that I am constructing a theorized spectator, one who sees something other than what Hall sees. Based on my repeated viewing of the seduction scene, I would assert that Berta Maria surrenders to Artinelli, and not entirely willingly. In the original version of the film, Artinelli appears much more threatening than romantic as he traps Berta Maria in his room. The title card makes it clear what Artinelli demands of her and why he thinks he deserves her affections: "I long for you. . . . Don't forget, without me you'd still be traveling around with the show people" (FWMS).[2] Under pressure, Berta Maria trades up, exchanging one man for a more sophisticated and successful one. The refusal to read Berta Maria as seduced rather than seducer persists into the 1990s. A recent video guide describes the film as a "[s]imple and tragic tale of the scheming young girl and the two men of whom she takes advantage" (Conners and Furtaw 1995, 965). But Artinelli also takes advantage of Berta Maria's youth and beauty at least as much as she takes advantage of him. Like the noir femme fatale, Berta Maria wants more than she has, more than "is appropriate to her status as a woman" (Place 1980, 46). Berta Maria's desire for social mobility, and her willingness to barter her body to obtain her goals, locates her far beyond the bounds of acceptable womanhood delineated by Huller's wife (and the video guide).

A certain sequence concerning Berta Maria deserves mention, since it is repeated twice in the course of the film, almost shot for shot. She and her new lover, Artinelli, have returned to their hotel from an evening rendezvous. The sequence begins in the hotel hallway, with a light shining at the end of the hall, over Berta Maria and Boss Huller's door. She and her lover embrace, and Berta Maria continues walking toward the end of the passageway. A cut ushers in the next shot, a close-up of

Berta Maria's face as she reapplies her powder before entering her room. The shot is disrupted as she raises the compact until it blocks her face, and in the next shot we see both her reflection in the compact mirror and her face as she freshens her lipstick. This sequence in *Variety* provides an early instance of a visual trope that will define femme fatales in Weimar cinema and film noir. As Place comments, "the many mirror shots in film noir . . . indicate women's duplicitous nature. They are visually split, thus not to be trusted" (Place 1980, 45–46). The femme fatale's intense interest in her own appearance also points, of course, to her narcissism. Certainly Berta Maria is constructing herself, fixing her image in order to allay Huller's suspicion, and to arouse his desire.

In the initial sequence, as Berta Maria enters their room, Huller sleeps on. When he awakens and questions her suspiciously, her construction of herself as desirable and innocent works perfectly. The screenplay, written by the director of the film, E. A. Dupont, describes Berta Maria's supposed effect on Huller in this sequence, suggesting that, "like a vampire, this woman had taken possession of him, and waves of lust and desire engulfed them both."[3] The second time the sequence plays out, Berta Maria's luck has run out. Although she makes the same effort to prepare herself for Huller's gaze, he is not in their room to behold her. Instead, aware of the betrayal, Huller waits in Artinelli's room and murders him.

At the end of *Variety*, Berta Maria sees the extent of the damage caused by the affair with Artinelli. In a scene of melodramatic excess, she attaches herself to Huller's massive form as he plods through the hotel passageway, intent on confessing to the murder. She tumbles and falls down the stairs screaming and crying. As Huller exits to the street and hails a cab to take him to the police station without looking back, the last shot of Berta Maria shows her motionless form head-down on the stairwell, both contained and imprisoned by the hotel doorway (fig. 2). Such a demise would not surprise Place: "The femme fatale ultimately loses physical movement, influence over the camera movement, and is often actually or symbolically imprisoned by composition as control over her is exerted and expressed visually: sometimes behind visual bars, . . . sometimes happy in the protection of a lover, . . . often dead, . . . sometimes symbolically rendered impotent" (Place 1980, 45). As I have shown, Berta Maria in *Variety*, and to a lesser degree, the prostitute in *The Street*, function as prototypical femme fatales. Similarly, the faithful if dull wives in both films serve as femmes attrapées, as visual and narrative foils to the alluring and dangerous "other" woman. The femme fatale's evolution from a prostitute whose actions are determined by her pimp to an autonomous and ambitious woman is one development traced in this study, both within the Weimar street film and into film noir. Another is the evolution of the femme attrapée from the stoic immobility she exhibits in *The Street* to the often restless defiance of the wife in film noir.

Like the femme attrapée and femme fatale in *Variety*, Huller

Figure 2. The motionless form in the stairwell—an excess of narrative and visual containment (*Variety*, 1925)

and Artinelli serve as foils for one another. The construction of the two male characters and the nature of each man's desirability function as another of the important stories *Variety* tells, especially to a female spectator. Hall describes Huller as "the hefty older man . . . a domesticated individual" (M. Hall 1926, 15:5). Berta Maria's life with Huller seems to require little of her beyond their trapeze act—he cooks, cleans, cuts her meat, and darns her stockings, all with an expression of blissful devotion. He is identified with the wives in the circus milieu, implicitly by his household tasks, and explicitly when he joins the other women in an early morning milk line. Huller seems to play the role of wife and lover to Berta Maria. But even early in the film, Huller's tender domesticity is tempered by his potentially threatening physical size and strength. In one early sequence, after a performance, Huller fans and dries Berta Maria playfully with a towel. Suddenly his expression changes from laughing to serious and, in a continuous close-up shot, his hand reaches out toward the camera and Berta Maria, blocking his face from view. The next shot, a close-up of Berta Maria's face, shows his hand pulling her head back. The sequence ends in a passionate embrace. Emil Jannings's bulk contributes to Huller's characterization and the actor's massive back plays a prominent role in many sequences of the film, including the murder scene and Berta Maria's final scene. Eisner lists the instances where Jannings's back dominates the screen and insists she tires "of this over-frequent 'back-acting'" (Eisner 1969, 280–81). In "Lulu and the Meter Man: Pabst's *Pandora's Box*," Thomas Elsaesser sees a similar visual quality in the frequent 'back-acting' of Fritz Kortner's portrayal of Dr. Schön (Elsaesser 1989, 47). For Elsaesser, the dynamism of the film comes from the "contrast between Lulu's agility . . . and the heavy, dark bulk of the men" (47). In *Variety*, Huller's physiognomy contrasts not only with Berta Maria's femininity, but also with a different sort of masculinity, that of the tall, slender, fine-boned Artinelli.

Artinelli differs from Huller in more than physiognomy. Although Huller also abandons his wife in favor of Berta Maria, Artinelli's pursuit of her appears contrived by comparison.

Artinelli maneuvers the stages of the seduction like a well-planned campaign. Like Berta Maria, the female object of desire in the film, Artinelli lazes in bed and makes himself up in the mirror both before and after his trapeze performances, apparently constructing his desirability. While both Huller and Artinelli elicit the gaze of the textually inscribed female spectators, neither fits neatly into Petro's categories for male figures in Weimar cinema. While Huller may have become the "impotent, self-punishing and frequently sadistic male" by the end of his misadventures, he remains vibrantly potent throughout them (Petro 1989, 155). And Artinelli, although eroticized, exhibits an agency that escapes "the passive and eroticized male" (157). Neither Huller nor Artinelli can be neatly categorized.

In his essay on sexual, social, and cinematic discourses in Weimar film, Richard McCormick identifies Artinelli as a "slender, sophisticated (and feminized), cosmopolitan man" (McCormick 1993, 651). McCormick, as I mention earlier, traces the male fear of otherness in Weimar film from the vampires and monsters of early Weimar cinema to the vamps of later Weimar film. He locates Artinelli on that continuum, somewhere between the two. McCormick never defines the term *feminized*, although he applies it to Nosferatu, Cesare (*The Cabinet of Dr. Caligari*), and Artinelli. The slender physiognomy of all three characters does not convey the same bulky masculinity as Emil Jannings's Huller. As I mentioned above, Artinelli does construct his image before a mirror, and he engages in duplicitous behavior. Perhaps these characteristics are what cause McCormick to call Artinelli feminized. In contrast to Artinelli, McCormick labels Huller "the good, solid German male," and "innocent hero" (651). I suspect many would have trouble reading Huller as an innocent hero, since he abandons his own wife in the opening reel of the film.[4] I also question Huller's good, solid German maleness. If we ignore for a moment his massive back and focus instead on his domestic prowess—his capabilities at the stove and with the darning needle—Huller might be seen to exhibit feminine characteristics as well. Artinelli is feminized along the lines of the duplicitous femme fatale; and

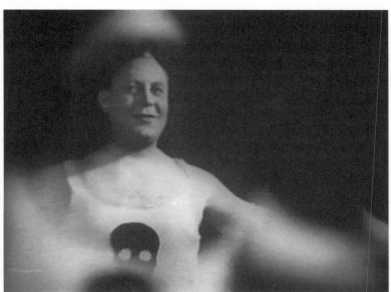

Figures 3–4. A diegetic female spectator gazes intently . . . and the object of her gaze (*Variety*, 1925)

Huller is feminized along the lines of the wife, willingly engaged in necessary domestic tasks.[5] While both characters engage in behavior or accomplish tasks that might be considered feminized, I prefer to say these characters offer the spectator a choice of masculinities, and give expression to the variegated nature of desire, especially for a heterosexual female spectator.[6]

Variety deals with both the private lives of its characters and public performances of the artists and acrobats. Spectacle, the act of seeing and of being seen, stands as one of the overt themes of the film. As McCormick notes, the film even features "a 'fantastic' collage . . . of eyes watching the spectacle" (McCormick 1993, 651). One sequence in particular addresses the nature of heterosexual desire in the public realm, portraying both Huller's bulky manliness and Artinelli's aloof sophistication as equally desirable. Berta Maria, Huller, and Artinelli stand on the stage after a performance, eliciting the fascinated and desiring gazes of various individuals in the audience. The sequence begins with a medium shot of a bejeweled and fur-clad woman, apparently gazing intently at the stage. She raises her glasses to her eyes (fig. 3). The next shot shows the view through one of the lenses of her glasses. Huller's smiling face and massive chest and shoulders are in clear focus in the round lens, while everything outside the lens but in the frame remains blurred (fig. 4). A cut takes us back to the woman, still intently looking through her glasses as she smiles expansively. The next shot shows a well-dressed man clapping emphatically as his eyes all but pop out of his head (fig. 9). He looks, the camera reveals, at Berta Maria, her whole body taking up the medium long shot as she bows and smiles (fig. 10). Next, a laughing, portly woman raises her opera glasses (fig. 5). A cut to the next shot shows Artinelli as the object of her gaze. A round iris pans quickly up his body and stops with a close-up of Artinelli's face and long neck (fig. 6). A final woman claps enthusiastically, and then looks disgustedly toward her husband, dozing in his chair (figs. 7 and 8). She looks back at the stage and resumes her clapping. This brief sequence accentuates two very different forms of male desirability, and I assert, through the textually

Figures 5–6. Another female spectator, another desiring gaze . . . and the object of her desires (*Variety*, 1925)

Figures 7–8. The static male counterpart to the dull wife . . . and his disgusted spouse (*Variety*, 1925)

Figures 9–10. A male spectator, his eyes popping out of his head . . . and the alluring object of his look (*Variety*, 1925)

inscribed spectators, admits the necessity of addressing hetero-sexual female desire, as well as male desire, in various permuta-tions. The brief scene showing the disaffected wife suggests, however momentarily, that the possibly dull and immobile wife has an equally static male counterpart. While I am not suggest-ing that *Variety* appeals only to female desires, or attempts to tell only the story of the wife bored by the husband, this se-quence certainly admits those possibilities.

The various sections of *Variety* I focus on are not the se-quences that attracted earlier critics. According to Fred Gehler, *Variety* was the most successful film in Germany in 1925 (Gehler 1993, 122). For *New York Times* critic Mordaunt Hall, *Variety* was not only one of the ten best pictures in the United States in 1926, but no film in 1927 surpassed it. (M. Hall 1928, 7:1). While *The Street* achieved its sophisticated effects with an immobile camera by varying the focal length and duration of shots, and through a diversity of editing techniques, in *Variety* the camera is cut loose from its moorings. Karl Freund, the di-rector of photography for *Variety*, also contributed to the Weimar classics *The Last Laugh* (*Der letzte Mann*, 1924), *Metropolis* (1927), and *Berlin, Symphony of a Great City* (1928), among other films. Later, in Hollywood, Freund won an Academy Award for the photography of *The Good Earth* (1937), and made a number of films noirs, including *Key Largo* (1948).[7] In *Variety*, as Eisner notes, "the camera, operated by the great Karl Freund, volup-tuously follows the agile forms as they leap forward and fly through space, turning over and over in daring somersaults" (Eisner 1969, 284). But it does not only follow the forms from below. Kaes supplements Eisner's description: "*Variety* provides silent attractions that speculate on the visual pleasure of the au-dience. The camera, high over the heads of the spectators, swings back and forth with the trapeze itself. Lights become blended points and lines and the film takes on an abstract qual-ity—a self-sufficient, sensual play of light and movement in the optical sphere" (Kaes 1993, 84).[8] *Variety* offers the filmgoer the spectacle of the circus and the crime melodrama as only cinema can, from the point of view of the performers in both dramas.

We see the audience in the Berlin Wintergarten from the perspective of performers on the trapeze. We imagine, with Huller, what it would be like to drop Artinelli in the course of the trapeze act, and look down from the heights on his broken form.[9] With *Variety*, cinema moves from motionless observation to confidential interaction, and the popularity of the movie suggests film audiences appreciated this new intimacy.

While the popularity of *Variety* is easily documented, deciding which version of the film a critic might have based her or his discussion upon remains almost impossible. There appear to be at least three versions of *Variety*. Most descriptions of the film, including Kracauer's, Gehler's, and Hall's, suggest it begins with the prison scene I describe, creating a frame for the story of Huller's ruin.[10] Another version, which includes a prison scene at the end of the film but not at the beginning, also exists (FWMS). The third version of the film changes the narrative drastically. This version, available on video in the United States, seems to follow the story as described by Herbert Ihering in the *Berliner Börsen-Courier* in 1925 (FWMS). In this version, Huller does not leave his wife for Berta Maria—instead he is married to her. Artinelli breaks up a happy marriage, not a pair of lovers, and Huller becomes the pitiful betrayed husband instead of a man who engineers his own ruin. In this version of the film, which also begins and ends with a prison scene, Huller's friends, and not his wife, petition for his early release. One explanation for the many versions of *Variety* might be that the filmmakers intentionally cobbled together various versions of the story, more to utilize extra footage than to please any certain audience. In any case, although I used the Video Yesteryear version of the film for the close readings presented in this analysis of *Variety*, the rendition of the narrative that features both the femme attrapée (however briefly) and the femme fatale is the film I consider to be on the continuum that connects the Weimar street film to film noir.

Most critics view female characters in film noir relative to male characters or to the male spectator in the cinema audience, or to both. Let me reiterate a point I made earlier. I do not deny the plausibility of a reading of film noir, or Weimar film before it, as male-centered. What I am suggesting is that the female spectator may not have read the women in Weimar street films or films noirs as reflections of unstable masculinity. For them, and for me (as a late-twentieth-century, white, heterosexual, academic, movie-loving feminist), these female characters might contain meaning totally separate from their status as the embodiment of male fears about women. Even though my argument runs counter to most critical work on Weimar cinema and film noir, the evidence for it is plain.

Female Agency and Its Lack
The Femme Fatale Gains (Possible) Admittance in *Asphalt*

I N *Asphalt,* one of the top ten films in Germany in 1929 (Garn-carz 1993, 199),[1] female characters undergo a sea change when compared to representations of women in the first Weimar street film, *The Street.* In the introduction to *Women in Film Noir,* E. Ann Kaplan notes how "[f]ilm noir is particularly notable for its treatment of women" (1978, 2). According to Kaplan, "the film noir world is one in which women are central to the intrigue of the films" (2). In much of film noir and in *Asphalt,* women's agency—their ability to mold and shape the events of the narrative—sets them apart from the wives, mothers, and prostitutes in other types of films, where the women "simply provide the background for the ideological work of the film which is carried out through men" (2). I have identified the femme attrapée as one attribute of Weimar street film and film noir. A character who might be described as a femme attrapée appears in *Asphalt.* She occupies the domestic realm and functions as wife and mother. But instead of stoically accepting the yoke of domestic drudgery as other femmes attrapées do, this character seems to thrive in her role as homemaker. There are risks involved in venturing outside the domestic realm, however, and the femme attrapée takes those risks. In my view the agency exhibited by these female characters—the femme attrapée who performs a revolutionary narrative function, and the femme fatale—may have made *Asphalt* an especially gratifying visual and narrative pleasure for the female spectator.

No doubt the film's technical virtuosity also added to its popular appeal. Eric Pommer, producer of many great Weimar films, including *The Cabinet of Dr. Caligari, Variety, The Last Laugh*, and *Metropolis*, had just returned from a stay in Hollywood when he undertook production of *Asphalt*.[2] The bustling street scenes that begin the film and intercut the action throughout were filmed in UFA's giant studio at Neubabelsberg, outside Berlin. Architect Erich Kettelhut constructed "reality" out of paper and glue in a huge studio for *Asphalt*.[3] According to Peter Mänz, Kettelhut offered various Berlin businesses the opportunity to finance their appearance on this street of dreams, the ultimate form of product placement (Mänz n.d., 9).[4] According to Mänz, Kettelhut's memoirs suggest the 230-meter-long street would have needed to be three times as long to accommodate all the firms requesting a place (8–9). Actual double-decker buses and scores of automobiles, carriages, and extras made the studio-constructed sets into a bustling urban vision. According to Anton Kaes, *Asphalt*, like earlier street films, used the street as an emblem for the problematic experience of modern urban life: "The milieu of the street, but in the service of symbolic excess; realism as a thoroughly thought-out construct, an especially difficult task in the studio" (Kaes 1993, 61).[5] Kaes's reaction would have pleased producer Pommer, who said of *Asphalt*, "the street then becomes a symbol of human existence—an unending merging of destinies" (quoted in Jacobsen et al. 1993, 61).[6]

Asphalt's technical brilliance was not limited to the impressive construction of a street milieu in a studio. The film opens with a sequence that recalls the energetic montages of *The Symphony of a Great City*. With the help of heavy tools, workers pound out and roll over fresh asphalt. The word ASPHALT appears, stamped out, letter by lighted letter, onto the pavement. These scenes usher in a montage of street shots, many from a dog's-eye view, of automobile wheels, streetcars, and bicycles rolling by, and the lower legs of pedestrians hurrying along. The sequence ends with a crescendo of music and images, the camera seeming to tumble and twirl around as one shot rapidly transitions to the next. This series of street-related, abstract superimpositions gives way to seamless continuity editing as the story begins to unfold. For Michael Hanisch, *Asphalt* documents the high art of the silent film in its final stages (Hanisch 1993, 182).[7] French critics Borde, Bauche, and Courtade agree: "There is nothing more modern than the amazing liveliness of the street scenes: the camera rules, chooses, isolates, works like the human eye, with tremendous awareness. . . . In 1927 the silent film achieved its great classical style. No more dead spaces, no more theater: the cinema was capable of everything."[8] The lively jazz sound track adds to the film's modern ambience.[9] Despite *Asphalt's* popular success and technical ingenuity, it was not uniformly praised.

In March 1929, Siegfried Kracauer laments, "It is too bad that, as so often happens in Germany, technical knowledge thrives at the price of intellectual awareness. This also occurs in *Asphalt*" (Kracauer 1929, 42).[10] Similarly scathing in 1969, Lotte Eisner suggests that director Joe May "seems to have been outclassed by techniques whose potency exceeded his own small talent" (Eisner 1969, 268). Eisner calls the plot insipid (267), while Kracauer suggests it would be suitable material for a trashy novel (Kracauer 1929, 42). Certainly the concern for class that dominated *The Street* and perhaps raised it above the level of the trivial in some eyes has disappeared from *Asphalt*. But *Asphalt* breathes life into the figure of the femme attrapée and fire into the femme fatale.

Although the female characters provide much of the emotional and physical force that drives the narrative, as with many films noirs, critics uniformly describe the plot as a masculine scenario. *Asphalt* does tell the story of young police officer Holk, played by the handsome Gustav Fröhlich, who is seduced by a beautiful jewel thief, Else, played by Betty Amann. Holk inadvertently kills Else's lover in a fistfight and is arrested by his own father, also a police officer. Else provides eyewitness testimony that frees Holk from jail, but she also confesses to her own thievery and is imprisoned. In the final moments of the film, Holk promises to wait for her. This sketch of the plot of

Asphalt does not account for the tenderness that imbues the Holk's familial relationships or the physical prowess of Else.

Asphalt, like *The Street* and *Variety,* contrasts the home with the street milieu and the figure of the wife, or femme attrapée, with the femme fatale. Early in the film, immediately following the montage of street images described above, the spectator enters the Holk household. The sequence, accompanied by gentle, marchlike music, begins with a shot of a caged bird. The camera pans up to jars of preserves high on a shelf, over to the wall clock ticking away the minutes, past the father's police helmet, which hangs on the wall, to Holk's father casually smoking a cigar and sipping a cup of coffee as the bespectacled mother reads aloud from the newspaper, commenting on the many things that happen in just one day.[11] A cut to Holk reveals him dressing for work, and checking his uniform in the mirror. He enters the drawing room, kisses his mother, and puts on his white gloves as both parents watch him proudly. He then chases his mother playfully down the hallway and leaves the flat. The father gets down his accounts and the camera returns to the caged bird. Suddenly automobiles appear to bear down on the caged bird from the four corners of the frame, and the lively street theme music takes over. After shots of rushing traffic, we see a close-up of Holk's glove-clad hand. The camera pulls back to show Holk standing in the middle of a bustling street directing traffic, and the next sequence begins.

As my verbal description of this seamlessly edited visual sequence shows, it contains all the components of the dull middle-class existence that the protagonists of *The Street* and *Variety* sought to escape. The caged bird, which also appears in *Variety,* cannot escape the confines of its prison any more than the Holk family can free itself from the restrictions of class, profession, and gender that the police helmet and the jars of preserves evoke.[12] The clock on the wall marks each slowly passing hour in this domestic space. Despite these tropes, the atmosphere in the Holk household defies the convention that requires the middle-class home be a bastion of stifling immobility. The husband and wife seem capable of meaningful interaction, and a sense of mutual love and respect defines their relationship with their son. While the home does not offer the enticements of the street, it appears as a nurturing, loving safe haven from the world outside, a safe haven with boundaries that prove dangerously permeable by the end of the film. The wife, in this film the mother of the protagonist, although responsible for the food on the family table, is not immobilized by her duties. She, like her husband and son, proves capable of actions outside the bounds of the family drawing room or kitchen. As noteworthy as the wife/mother's actions are, her mobility pales in comparison to the forceful physicality of the femme fatale in *Asphalt*.

Although the femme fatale eventually takes center screen, in the early sequences of the film the camera chooses to show various depictions of women in the modern, urban milieu. I want to touch on possible readings of these sequences, especially by the female spectator of *Asphalt*. To do so, we must return to Holk, whom we left directing traffic on a busy evening street. Suddenly, a beautifully clad young woman bumps up onto the curb in her automobile. Directing traffic around her, Holk straightens the giant teddy bear (!) sitting next to her in the passenger's seat, calms the angry male drivers who have been held up, and aids her in getting back onto the street. Narratively, this scene works as a proof of Holk's professional detachment in the face of feminine beauty. But it also portrays women as part of the hustle and bustle of the city street, not neatly tucked away and contained in homes and offices.

Next the camera pans from Holk up to the streetlights, which turn on one by one. It moves fluidly up the street, watching the flux of well-dressed people walking by. It stops to watch a woman removing her stockings in a shop window. A crowd of men and women watch with expressions of pleasure and admiration. For one woman in the crowd of people outside the shop window, the gratification of purchasing the stockings will have to be forestalled. In the crowd of men and women watching the display, two male pickpockets successfully steal her wallet from her purse. Hales, with her focus on the woman as sexual crim-

inal, sees this as an invitation to the spectator to "make a connection between female sexuality (the sensual act of brushing a
silk stocking against the skin) and common criminality" (Hales
1996, 113). Just as Hales implies more agency than I see in the
portrayal of the prostitute in *The Street,* she reads even innocent
female characters as criminal, or potentially so. Hales neglects
to point out that in this sequence in *Asphalt,* a woman clearly remains the victim of male criminals. A similar persistence of vision affects the reading of women in Weimar cinema and film
noir as commodities.

Certainly the shop window display positions the live model
and the stockings as commodities. For both the diegetic and
extradiegetic male spectators, it offers a similar sensual pleasure
in looking at a desirable object.[13] But the female spectators,
both diegetic or in the film audience, are positioned as both the
objects and subjects of commodity exchange, in a sense encouraged to reproduce themselves as objects. The female spectator must purchase the black silk stockings in order to make
herself the desirable object of the male gaze.

In *Star Gazing,* Jackie Stacey problematizes these "mutually
reinforcing relations of powerlessness" by suggesting that consumption can be "a site of negotiated meanings, of resistance,
and of appropriation as well as of subjection and exploitation"
(Stacey 1994, 185, 187). Stacey shows how for British women
in the 1950s, the Hollywood version of American femininity
transgressed a "restrictive British femininity" (198). According
to Stacey, consumption became a strategy of resistance and
"the consumption of commodities connected to Hollywood
stars can be seen as a rejection of, or an opposition to, the domestic roles of self-sacrificing wife and mother" (220). The
woman in the display window cannot and should not be recast
as an instance of resistance to female subjection in patriarchal
culture. But Stacey's view of the consumption of certain commodities as an opposition to the domestic roles available to a
woman does provide a possible avenue of pleasure for the female spectator, and one that does not necessarily imply maso-
chism. In addition, femininity and consumption are not linked

only at the level of commodity tie-ins. Viewing the purchase of a film or the admission to the theater as a commodity, I see the purchase of the forms of femininity offered by *Asphalt* and in Hollywood films noirs as also resisting the alternative roles of self-sacrificing wife and mother, often with a vengeance. The femme fatale in *Asphalt* certainly offers a vibrant alternative.

To introduce her, the camera crosses the street, observing traffic and people from a view slightly higher than the human eye. It approaches a jewelry store window and catches a glimpse of Else, the femme fatale, inside the shop. The visual pleasure provided by the seamless sequence described above is exceeded only by the narrative potential of each by-play the camera records. Next, a cut takes us inside the store. A white-bearded salesman flirts with Else as he shows her various diamonds, while she extravagantly accepts his attentions.

From the moment she is introduced, Else demands the attention of salesman, camera, and spectator. Sultry horn music serves as her thematic accompaniment. She wears a light colored, form-fitting satin gown with a collar of fur. She stands out against the gray and black tones of the jewelry shop and street. A brilliant white hat frames her face and accentuates her dark hair and eyes. Mordaunt Hall calls actress Betty Amann, who plays Else, captivating but notes "her eyelashes are made-up as if for the musical comedy stage" (M. Hall 1930, 33:4). For Frieda Grafe and Enno Patalas, Else's artificial lashes contribute to the atmosphere of decadent excess which seduces Holk: "The power of the state is gratifyingly corrupted by elegance, by furs, by satin fabrics, by the velvet atmosphere of a boudoir and a glance under false eyelashes. One senses it is the eyes that are seduced" (Grafe and Patalas 1969, 175).[14] Else is so successful in her captivation of the white-bearded salesman that once he has recovered the diamond she stole, he actually asks Holk to release her. Holk responds that as an official *(Beamter)*, he must do his duty and take her to the police station. But when Holk attempts to do this Else turns the full force of her seductive arsenal upon him.

In the taxi on the way to the station Else cries copiously,

asks him for a handkerchief, and tells Holk she attempted to steal the diamond because her rent was due and she is desperately afraid she will end up on the street. Else throws herself around Holk's neck and pleads with him to allow her to go to her apartment to get her papers. Holk forcefully pushes her off, straightens his collar, and agrees. Having won this small victory, a relieved Else sizes up her opponent and surreptitiously makes herself up in her compact. Else's duplicitous nature, like Berta Maria's in *Variety*, is not hidden from the spectator. Once she and Holk are inside Else's luxurious apartment one particular shot deserves mention. According to Eisner, "[i]n order to portray Fröhlich's (Holk's) embarrassment in the flighty woman's drawing-room, Joe May just shows two straddled legs clad in thick leather gaiters above a pair of enormous boots" (Eisner 1969, 267). This shot does contrast the soft, sensual textures associated with Else and her dwelling with the shiny black leather of the boots (fig. 11). But for me, instead of indicating Holk's embarrassment this shot seems emblematic of male physical prowess and societal authority. Those boots may not belong in the drawing room but their presence and authoritative posture indicate the power vested in the man who wears them. Else cannot vanquish those boots with anything less than a full-throttle frontal attack.

Instead of getting her papers from her apartment, Else climbs into bed, pulls the silken covers up to her neck and refuses to get up. Incensed, Holk threatens to call an ambulance to take her to the police station. As he picks up the telephone, Else, now clad in tight, black lace pajamas, springs from her bed, runs to the drawing room and rips the telephone cord from the wall, throwing the phone to the carpet. Holk threatens her with a fist and she attacks him, throwing herself at him and wrapping her arms firmly around his neck. He throws her bodily to the floor. Else leaps up like an acrobat and jumps on Holk, wrapping her legs around his body (fig. 12). Suddenly, still attached to him as though she is a child climbing a tree, Else pulls back. She eyes Holk lustfully. "You please me,"[15] Else tells Holk, as she embraces him (fig. 13). Holk continues to

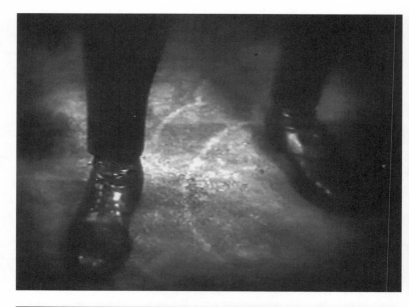

Figures 11–12. Male authority in the drawing room, but the femme fatale has her way (*Asphalt*, 1929)

Figures 13–14. She actively seduces the object of her desires . . . and vanquishes the boots as well (*Asphalt*, 1929)

protest and seeks to remove her arms from around·his neck, but is apparently unsuccessful. She knocks his police helmet to the floor, runs her hands through his hair, and kisses him. The sequence closes with a shot of Else's bare feet sliding up and down the black leather boots (fig. 14), and finally, a pan to Holk's helmet on the carpet. For Hales, that shot "represents the powerlessness of the law vis-à-vis the sexual woman as criminal" (Hales 1996, 114). But the sequence might also represent a woman who has obtained the object of her desire and prevented herself from being turned over to the police. Else proves more than a match for Holk, despite his official status as male representative of patriarchal power.

Shortly after Else has successfully seduced Holk, the camera focuses its attention on him in a way that emphasizes his physical desirability to the heterosexual female spectator. Petro discusses the potential pleasure, specifically for the Weimar female spectator, of "contemplating male passivity" when an

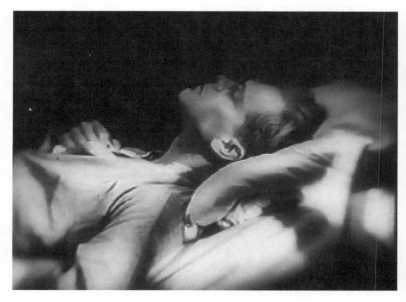

Figure 15. The man as passive object of desire (*Asphalt*, 1929).

"eroticized male figure claims attention within the visual field" (Petro 1989, 199). In the films Petro discusses this is usually accomplished on the narrative level by the illness or exhaustion of the male protagonist. Holk cannot be associated with male passivity at this level. He is the picture of youthful physical health. Almost the only way Holk can appear as a passive and eroticized object of the camera's and spectator's gaze is in his sleep. In a sequence that takes place after Else has had her way with him, crosscutting takes us from a shot of Holk, half-undressed, sleeping on his bed at home, to a shot of Else giggling and joking with her maid as she bathes at her apartment. A medium close-up of Holk's handsome sleeping face and broad shoulders reveals his undershirt beneath his unbuttoned shirt (fig. 15). This crosscutting, or "editing that alternates shots of two or more lines of action occurring in different places, usually simultaneously," highlights Holk as the passive object of desire (Bordwell and Thompson 1993, 493). Indeed, the two shots of Holk sleeping have more than a passing similarity to the shots Petro uses as examples of male passivity from the film *Refuge* (Petro 1989, 193, 198). Holk is offered as "an object of sexual stimulation through sight" for the heterosexual female viewer (Mulvey 1989, 18). According to Mulvey, "the male cannot bear the burden of sexual objectification" because man "is reluctant to gaze at his exhibitionist like" (20), but in *Asphalt* he must bear the burden, however briefly. My point here is that *Asphalt* plays specifically to the heterosexual female spectator, providing her with pleasures that may even be offered at the expense of the heterosexual male spectator.

When I first viewed this film at the Friedrich Wilhelm Murnau Stiftung in Wiesbaden, I suspect my delighted whoop at Else's physical seduction of Holk echoed through the hallway outside the screening room. Only Hales makes any reference to Else's aggressiveness, despite its shocking quality. Borde, Bauche, and Courtade do call the seduction scene "a true cinematic model" (Borde et al. 1969, 176).[16] If the roles were reversed and Holk had seduced Else as aggressively as she does him, I would have undoubtedly called it something other than seduction. Holk's firm and steadfast refusal of her attentions might well qualify him as a victim. But the shock of seeing a woman physically attack a man, launch herself at him, and have her way with him, was undeniably pleasurable for me and I suspect this pleasure might also have been experienced by women in the Weimar film audience. Audiences go into movie theaters with a certain set of expectations that films must gratify to keep spectators satisfied. But the denial or subversion of expectations provides an equally powerful tool for enticing audiences to return, especially if the film narrative only delays gratification of established expectations.

In film noir, and in *Asphalt*, the femme fatale exhibits her power and agency only to be recontained in the final reel. In explaining feminist critical interest in film noir, Janey Place suggests that "it stands as the only period in American film in which women are deadly but sexy, exciting and strong" (Place 1980, 54). Else does seem more like the femmes fatales of film noir than her Weimar cohorts, Lulu in *Pandora's Box*, and Lola Lola in *The Blue Angel*. Both Lulu and Lola Lola, like Else, are presented as objects of desire, important because of their "to-be-looked-at-ness" (Mulvey 1989, 19). While Else may not initially be the object of Holk's desire, she functions as the object of the camera's interest from her first appearance on the screen. But unlike Lulu and Lola Lola, there is nothing ambiguous about Else's agency. Not only an object of desire, Else backs up her own desires, her own choice of sexual object, with emphatic action.[16]

Not surprisingly, Else ends up behind bars at the end of *Asphalt*. In order to clear Holk of the murder of her lover, she admits her own complicity—that she is a jewel thief and her murdered lover a wanted criminal. But before she makes this confession at the police station, Else climbs the stairs to the Holk's dwelling and is admitted to the apartment by his mother. As I pointed out earlier, for Petro the singular motif that addresses the female audience in Weimar cinema is that of the "female figure [who] stands outside a locked and closed door and begins knocking, then pounding, as if to express an ineffable desire and anger" (Petro 1989, 218). I agree with Petro that this is a dominant image in Weimar melodramas. Yet in *Asphalt*, Else knocks on the door of middle-class stability and domesticity and is, however reluctantly, admitted—a startling change. Holk's mother brings Else to the police station and bursts into the examination room to insist Else be heard. As Kracauer notes, "[h]ere the street penetrates the bourgeois parlour" (Kracauer 1947, 158).[18] According to Kracauer, "two dimensions of life [are] interrelated which in Grune's *The Street* had been incompatible with each other" (158).

In the final moments of *Asphalt*, as his parents look on, Holk embraces Else passionately and promises to wait for her. He watches as the barred doors close on her and she walks away down the prison hallway, accompanied by a policeman.[19] For Hales, the metal grate that separates Holk and Else symbolizes "the difference in their true natures. The bourgeois man is different from and at the same time linked to the criminal woman in his desire for her" (Hales 1996, 115). Hales sees Else as the representation of "pure evil" (115). But Else sacrifices herself to ensure Holk's freedom, and pays the price for both Holk's and her own criminality. Speaking in terms of masculine identity, Kracauer suggests "that by implying that the bonds between the prostitute and her bourgeois lover will survive the latter's submission," *Asphalt*, and other street films like it, fundamentally change the meaning of that submission (Kracauer 1947, 160).[20] Instead of indicating a "resumption of authoritarian behavior," it marks "an event of far-reaching consequence" (160). Kracauer refers to Holk's submission to the authority of his father and the state, after his initial rebellion, a rebellion which is expressed by Holk's not taking Else to the police station early in the narrative. Kracauer only discusses Holk's submission, although the film ends with Else submitting to the same authority and with more painful results.

Yet, in a sense, I agree with Kracauer. Holk's submission does differ from that of the rebellious philistine in *The Street* and Huller's in *Variety*. He does not reject his lover from the streets in order to beat a hasty retreat to the safety of domesticity. But more interesting for me and more important for the female spectator in Weimar Germany are the female characters. In *Asphalt* the street does penetrate the drawing room; the wife and the femme fatale come face to face and work together toward a common goal. The wife is not a voiceless, lifeless form that anchors the dull domesticity of the bourgeois home; she is a vibrant member of an apparently loving family. And the femme fatale does not follow the whims of the men surrounding her but actively and with an impressive physicality determines her future and pursues the object of her desires. *Asphalt* leaves open the possibility that Else, despite her impressive agency, might live happily ever after. The desperate and emphatic insistence on containment of female desire and agency we see expressed over and over again in film noir and much of Weimar cinema is dealt with more ambiguously in *Asphalt*. It seems to me that both versions of femininity offered to the female spectator by *Asphalt* have their attractions and their liberating potential; and the narrative itself, by virtue of its ambiguity, seems to support that liberation.

Prototype Noir: *M* as Film Noir?

Thrillers are a venerable type in the films. But the current vogue is unique in its predilection for familiar, everyday surroundings as the setting in which crime and violence occur. . . . the emphasis many recent productions place, [is] not so much on outright sadism, as on the permanent menace of it. Apprehension is accumulated; threatening allusions and dreadful possibilities evoke a world in which everybody is afraid of everybody else, and no one knows when or where the ultimate and inevitable horror will arrive. When it does arrive it arrives unexpectedly: erupting out of the dark from time to time in a piece of unspeakable brutality.
—Siegfried Kracauer

In his 1946 essay "Hollywood's Terror Films: Do They Reflect an American State of Mind?" Siegfried Kracauer examines

Hollywood's film noir and decides that these dark films do reflect "an inherent concern with mental disintegration" (Kracauer 1946, 134).[21] Kracauer recognizes the milieu of the film noir, noting that "shots of street life were also prominent in German films of the pre-Hitler Weimar Republic period that described the tragedies of instinct-possessed beings" (134). Kracauer is not the only theorist to note the connections between Weimar cinema and film noir. In his study of German expressionist film, John Barlow suggests that the Weimar crime film *M* (Fritz Lang, 1931) "shows traces of expressionism that occur later in the American films of the 1940s, particularly those black and white films dealing with a dark urban world of crime and corruption, called 'film noir'" (Barlow 1982, 187). According to Barlow, "*M* uses expressionistic devices to externalize fear and madness, setting the standards for the thrillers and criminal dramas of the later American cinema" (186). Barlow refers to the visual style of *M* and sees expressionistic features in the looming shadow of Elsi Beckmann's murderer, which appears menacingly across a notice announcing a reward for information leading to the arrest of a child murderer, and in the "shadowy darkness of [the murderer's] hiding place in a loft . . . where he looks like a caged animal" (186). Others go so far as to identify *M* as the first film noir, citing the film's urban setting and atmosphere of fear and paranoia. Silver and Ward include the 1951 American version of *M*, "an almost exact remake of the Fritz Lang film," although it takes place in Los Angeles, in their encyclopedic reference to film noir (Silver and Ward 1992, 178).[22] Fritz Lang, who directed *M* as well as numerous Hollywood films noirs including *The Big Heat*, which I discuss in depth later, was one of many German artists who fled to the United States in the 1930s and 1940s, providing a stylistic link between the Weimar film industry and film noir. According to Thomas Schatz, directors like Lang, as well as "Ernst Lubitsch, F. W. Murnau, . . . Billy Wilder, Douglas Sirk, and E. A. Dupont along with countless technicians, screenwriters and performers . . . complemented Hollywood's traditional obsession with plot and dialogue with a heightened concern with set design, composition, and camerawork" (Schatz 1981, 113).

M does exhibit stylistic elements that reappear in film noir, but *M* also reiterates and develops on a thematic level the ambivalent relationship between women and the domestic realm present in the Weimar street film. In the street films, the portrayal of the home develops from a vision of safe, if stupefying domesticity to a portrayal of the home as vulnerable to the potentially disruptive forces of the street. Instead of the man of the house venturing out onto the street and then returning home, the street dwellers themselves threaten the domestic realm. In *M*, Elsi Beckmann's mother resembles the wife in *The Street* and even prepares dinner with the same loving attention, although unlike the husband in the earlier film, Elsi is denied the opportunity of returning to the safety of her home. The lurking danger of the street, embodied by the child murderer, literally snatches Elsi from her mother's waiting arms. The

Figure 16. The backbreaking labors of the domestic realm (*M*, 1931)

tragedy of Elsi Beckmann's death, reinforced by her mother's voice calling Elsi's name in empty, shadow-filled stairwells, is further intensified by the spectator's knowledge that the mother's only apparent joy has been horrifically choked out. The domestic realm, once a safe haven, appears mortally threatened by the forces of evil that surround it.

The external threat of the child murderer does not represent the only evil in the life of Elsi Beckman's mother. Although she resembles the wife of the rebellious philistine of *The Street*, Elsi's mother appears exhausted and overworked, a virtual slave to endless amounts of laundry, and she commiserates with a similarly overworked neighbor woman (fig. 16). The domestic realm is explicitly portrayed as a province of endless, back-breaking labor, and a locus for the femme attrapée. Even as external dangers bear down on familial settings, the need for female characters to escape their prison of domestic drudgery increases. As we shall see, film noir elaborates on the external threats and simultaneously reiterates the trap the domestic realm presents for female characters.

PART THREE
Film Noir Contexts and Texts

The Noir Years
U.S. War and Postwar Culture and Cinema, 1941–1958

F ILM noir, like Weimar cinema, can be identified to a certain degree as a postwar phenomenon. During the Weimar Republic, as Germans sought to recover from total defeat in a war for which Germany was responsible, they suffered economic and political turmoil of epic proportions. Between 1941 and 1958, the years I have identified with film noir, the United States emerged from World War II victorious, gaining economic strength and settling into a period of prosperity and relative stability. Although I have problematized the gains in social mobility and political influence made by women in the Weimar years, the liberalism of Weimar Germany does stand in contrast to the increasing conservatism in the United States after World War II, particularly with regard to women. If the New Woman of Weimar Germany was, as Koonz suggests, young, middle-class, "employed, socially free and autonomous," the New Women in the post–World War II United States was middle-aged, middle-class, employed, and married (Koonz 1987, 42). Her employment made her a New Woman, but her emancipation was not legal, economic, or symbolic. The New Woman undergoes a transformation from youthful and radical in Weimar Germany to older and less ideologically threatening in the United States in the 1940s and 1950s.

William Chafe points out that World War II witnessed a 50 percent increase in the size of the female labor force in the United States (Chafe 1991, 121). According to Chafe, before

World War II, "in 1940, the percentage of women at work was almost exactly what it had been in 1910," and most of the jobs were menial or low paying (121). Women "rushed to war plants," eager to take advantage of the higher wages, while more than two million took jobs in offices (126–27). Just as they had during World War I in Germany, middle-class women in the United States who were unwilling or unable to work contributed to the war effort through volunteerism, flocking to Red Cross headquarters and Civilian Service Bureaus in the 1940s (125). After World War I in Weimar Germany, public opinion turned against working women. In the United States after World War II, returning "veterans took priority over wartime workers," "some employers revised their age requirements, throwing women over forty-five out of work," and large corporations like "IBM reimposed earlier restrictions on the hiring of wives" (158–59). Despite the forces aligned against them after the war in the United States, working women, like the Weimar women before them, managed to remain in or reenter the employment picture, albeit, as Chafe notes, in "sex-segregated and sex-typed occupations" (160).

The married, middle-aged, middle-class woman who had already fulfilled her culturally determined primary role, that of mother, became through her employment, "the crucial means by which many families achieved middle-class status" (Chafe 1991, 162). Her wages, like her work in the home, served to bolster and strengthen the family. Even the jobs women were likely to fulfill in "clerical, sales, [or] service positions," allowed women to be perceived as helpmates instead of competitors to their male coworkers (160). For Chafe, in the United States "everything in the social and cultural atmosphere militated against ideological and political confrontation and in support of accommodation to traditional values" (171). Women managed an apparent adherence to traditional values at the same time as they established themselves as an ever-increasing presence in the public sphere.

Just as the Nazis made motherhood a matter of national public policy in Germany, antifeminists in the United States advocated a similar agenda in the late 1940s. According to Chafe, Ferdinand Lundberg and Marynia Farnham, authors of the 1947 publication "Modern Woman: The Lost Sex," insisted that "[w]omen had been created to be biologically and psychologically dependent on the man" (Chafe 1991, 178). Lundberg and Farnham's proposals included a "government-sponsored propaganda campaign to bolster the family, . . . cash subsidies to encourage women to bear more children and annual awards to mothers who excelled at child rearing" (179). Many shared these beliefs and women's magazines like *McCall's* and *Ladies' Home Journal* advocated "the joys of 'femininity' and 'togetherness'" (179). In the United States, Lundberg and Farnham's conclusions were mediated somewhat by social scientists such as Margaret Mead. Based on her studies of South Sea cultures, Mead asserted, "There is no evidence that suggests women are naturally better at caring for children [than men]" (Chafe 1991, 182). In Nazi Germany, dissension might lead to elimination. In the United States democratic rule protected the middle-aged, middle-class woman who worked her way into the public realm from the virulent backlash to which her Weimar counterpart was eventually subjected. To a certain extent, Hollywood cinema other than film noir perpetuated a less ideologically threatening view of women. In the world of film noir, however, women were subject to a malignant backlash, often more brutal and fatal than those that afflicted the women in the Weimar street films I discuss.

Unlike Weimar cinema, no momentous historical events delineate film noir's beginning and end, although the term *film noir* was used by French cinema critics to describe a certain quality they noticed in some of the American films flooding the international market after World War II. According to Alain Silver and Elizabeth Ward, the critics identified the new dark cinema with the popular "Serie Noire" novels, translations of "the work of such authors as [Dashell] Hammett, [Raymond] Chandler, James M. Cain and Horace McCoy" (Silver and Ward 1992, 1).[1] As R. Barton Palmer notes in *Hollywood's Dark Cinema*, the hard-boiled literary tradition of these writers featured "grimly naturalistic stories about adultery, greed, murder and paranoia" (Palmer 1994, 7). Film noir translates these stories of ambiguity and duplicity into cinematic terms, just as the film *Nosferatu* did with Expressionism in Weimar Germany. Critics Raymond Borde and Etienne Chaumeton wrote the first book-length study of film noir published in 1955. They call the phenomenon a series, or "group of films from one country sharing common traits," and claim it begins in the early forties with *The Maltese Falcon* (1941), and ends in 1955 with *Kiss Me Deadly* (Silver and Ward 1992, 372).[2] In his "Notes on Film Noir," Paul Schrader expresses an opinion shared by numerous critics, suggesting film noir "can stretch at its outer limits from *The Maltese Falcon* to *Touch of Evil* (1958)" (Schrader 1972, 9). I agree that film noir begins in 1941, with some of its thematic conventions appearing in *The Maltese Falcon*, a film I will discuss in detail later. Another 1941 film, *Citizen Kane*, introduced the stylistic flourishes and complicated narrative structures that have become synonymous with film noir.[3] By 1958, in *Touch of Evil*, these stylistic flourishes become perversely exaggerated, reflecting the corruption and dissipation of one of film noir's favorite existential heroes, the hard-boiled detective. Locating film noir between two great works of U.S. cinema, both directed by Orson Welles, provides cohesion to my investigation.

The exact contents and contours of film noir undergo constant scrutiny by critics.[4] Film noir is often called a genre, defined by Bordwell and Thompson as a type of film "which audiences and filmmakers recognize by . . . familiar narrative conventions," for example a western or gangster film (Bordwell and Thompson 1993, 494). Those who view film noir as a genre often use the term without problematizing it or identify plot structures and character types—for example, detective yarns with hard-boiled heroes and femmes fatales—as generic film noir. I do not deny that many satisfying films noirs exist within the detective genre and I discuss two of them in depth here. But one of the most intriguing aspects of film noir is its transgeneric quality. *Mildred Pierce* (1945) functions as both a detective and a woman's picture, and Silver and Ward identify *My*

Darling Clementine (1946) and a number of other westerns as film noir (Silver and Ward 1992, 325). As Palmer points out, "[f]ilms noirs were understood and marketed as belonging to other genres—the detective film, the woman's picture, the thriller, and . . . the crime melodrama or mystery" (Palmer 1994, 6). Directors and producers in Hollywood did not initially set out to make films noirs; as I point out earlier, it was French critics who first noticed and named the phenomenon.

Some identify film noir as a style, similar to the German expressionist film discussed earlier. A style requires the "repeated and salient uses of film techniques [which becomes] characteristic of . . . a group of films" (Bordwell and Thompson 1993, 397). In "Some Visual Motifs of *Film Noir*," J. A. Place and L. S. Peterson define the visual style of film noir as antitraditional (Place and Peterson 1976). The dominant Hollywood lighting technique requires high-key lighting; film noir lighting is low-key. According to Place and Peterson: "[t]he ratio of key to fill light is great, creating areas of high contrast and rich black shadows . . . the low-key *noir* style opposes light and dark, hiding faces, rooms, urban landscapes—and, by extension, motivation and true character—in shadow and darkness which carry connotations of the mysterious and the unknown" (327; italics in original). The female protagonists in film noir were not photographed using soft-focus or diffuse lighting techniques. Instead, "noir heroines were shot in tough, unromantic close-ups of direct, undiffused light which create a hard, statuesque surface beauty that seems more seductive but less attainable, at once alluring and impenetrable" (328). Finally, according to Place and Peterson, film noir emphasized antitraditional mise en scène—instead of "harmonious triangular three-shots and balanced two-shots," film noir commonly features "bizarre off-angle compositions of figures placed irregularly in the frame, which create a world that is never stable or safe, that is always threatening to change drastically and unexpectedly" (333–35). For me the visual style defined by Place and Peterson delineates film noir. I agree with Thomas Schatz that "film noir was a system of visual and thematic conventions which were not associated with a specific genre, but with a cinematic style and historical period" (Schatz 1981, 113). In *The Classical Hollywood Cinema*, David Bordwell, Janet Staiger, and Kristen Thompson also discuss film noir's patterns of "nonconformity within Hollywood," and emphasize that films noirs were initially "defined chiefly by their difference from the mainstream Hollywood product" (Bordwell et al. 1985, 75). In brief, most film noir narratives take place in urban environments; rely on antitraditional, low-key lighting, camera work, and mise en scène to create an atmosphere of uncertainty and fear; and foreground female sexuality and duplicity.

From 1941 to 1958, Hollywood experienced more than the evolution of film noir. From 1934 until the mid-fifties, the content of movies remained under the strict and repressive supervision of the Production Code Administration. It seems amazing that film noir developed at all, considering that the code's strictures: "It was forbidden to show the details of a crime, or to display machine guns . . . or other illegal weapons, or to discuss weapons at all in dialogue scenes. It was further required that law enforcement officials never be shown dying at the hands of criminals and that all criminal activities within a given film were shown to be punished. Under no circumstances could a crime be shown to be justified" (Cook 1981, 267). In addition to working around the production code, filmmakers in Hollywood during the noir years saw major upheavals. They experienced the demise of the studio system, had their ranks decimated by the investigations of the House Un-American Activities Committee, and saw the advent of television, the first form of entertainment to compete successfully with the silver screen. According to Cook, the competition with television "resulted in Hollywood's rapid conversion from black-and-white to color production between 1952 and 1955" (413). It also caused a rush to develop wide-screen technologies to take advantage of the screen size advantage movies enjoy over television, and a craze for blockbusters like *War and Peace* and *The Ten Commandments* (both 1956).

Two popular fifties genres, the western and the science fiction film, according to James Monaco, "exhibited the downbeat mood of Film Noir, each in its own way" (Monaco 1981, 254). Monaco suggests that the "Western began to treat more serious and more pessimistic themes; the Science Fiction film developed a number of objective correlatives for the cultural paranoia of the decade" (254). While it would be fascinating to read the western and science fiction films of the fifties in terms of female subjectivity, as far as I know, that work remains to be done. Another type of film, however, has been read in terms of male subjectivity and postwar trauma, and casts an interesting light on my discussion of film noir.

According to Cook, in 1941 Hollywood created the War Activities Committee and began producing unsophisticated "propaganda and morale-boosting" films that "disappeared rapidly from the American screen when . . . an infinitely more authentic version of the war, contained in newsreels" confronted viewer (Cook 1981, 394). Next came documentaries, directed by major Hollywood directors, that "persuasively and unromantically explained the necessity of America's involvement in the war" (394). The postwar period also provides numerous examples of fictional films that seek to ameliorate the effects of the war.

For Kaja Silverman many of these postwar films require female characters to assume responsibility for disruptions in the social fabric caused by World War II (Silverman 1992). Silverman also sees male characters pervasively cast as victims, and asserts that female characters must "confer the phallus upon them [the male characters] by 'refusing' to see their inadequacy" (114). Silverman provides analyses of a number of postwar productions, and in each instance shows how the female characters take responsibility for the male characters' failings. *The Best Years of Our Lives* (1946) addresses the problems of peacetime, both for servicemen returning to civilian life after the war and for the communities to which they return. For Silverman, the film does not oblige "the female subject to display her lack to her sexual other," but "repeatedly calls upon her to look acceptingly at his—to acknowledge and embrace male castration" (69). One of the actors in the film, Harold Russell, actually lost his hands in the war. Russell plays a returning double amputee, a role for which he won two Academy Awards, one for best supporting actor and another for "bringing hope and courage to his fellow veterans" (Katz 1994, 1187).

Silverman also discusses *It's a Wonderful Life* (1946) and *The Guilt of Janet Aimes* (1947). *It's a Wonderful Life,* according to Silverman, "shows every male subject to be both indispensable and irreplaceable, and so attempts to neutralize the historical trauma of civilian reentry" (Silverman 1992, 93). *The Guilt of Janet Aimes* requires Janet, played by Rosalind Russell, to assume "sole responsibility not only for her husband's death [in the war], but for the weakening of the dominant fictions—for the loss of belief in the family, the American home, romantic love, and the phallic male subject" (117). What interests me about film noir is that, unlike the female characters in the postwar films Silverman takes as the objects of her study, the femme fatale refuses to play the role history and society seem to require. For that, as we shall see, she will pay.

As I mentioned earlier, female characters in film noir, as well as the Weimar street film, are persistently read relative to the male characters. In "No Way Out: Existential Motifs in the Film Noir," Robert Porfirio notes that "[t]he 'femme noire' was usually also a *femme fatale,* and a host of domineering women, castrating bitches, unfaithful wives and black widows seemed to personify the worst of male sexual fantasies" (Porfirio 1976, 216).[5] Each of the terms Porfirio uses to describe these femmes noirs implies a male victim, a man who is dominated, castrated, cheated on, or murdered by the woman in question. Considering the usual treatment of women in film noir and in some Weimar street films, it seems almost laughable that men should be so pervasively cast as victims. True to the pattern, Carl Richardson similarly type-casts the femme fatale, and even implies she deserves the violent end she usually receives: "film noir depicts spidery women answerable to a host of misdeeds and misadventures. Women connive, steal, and murder. They are not 'fallen women,' victimized by patriarchal exploitation.

They are fully responsible for their actions. They are ambitious exploiters, whose misdeeds merit punishment (in accordance to the Production Code), doled out in disappointment, grief, and sometimes . . . death" (Richardson 1992, 45). Again, the male victim lurks behind the description of spidery women. These women have the gall to ambitiously exploit, connive against, steal from, and murder men. Richardson boldly suggests the femme fatale has somehow successfully stepped outside patriarchal ideology. Instead of being victims of men they are victimizers (of men), and for that they must and will be punished. This vision of autonomous, strong women functioning outside patriarchal ideology certainly has its seductive side, especially for a female spectator. Unfortunately, as my discussion of women in Weimar street films and films noirs suggests, female characters might be resisting the oppression inherent in the patriarchy, but they are far from free of it.

Many writers, such as John Belton, see the antifeminist mood of film noir as a logical result of the changing roles of women in the United States:

> [T]he changing status of American women during the war and postwar period challenges male dominance. The entry of women into the workforce and their taking over of traditional male roles violate the fundamental order of sexual relations. . . . In leaving the private sphere of home and family to enter the public sphere of work, women . . . have abandoned—or at least neglected—the domestic needs of sweethearts, husbands, and/or children. Film noir dramatizes the consequences of this neglect, transforming women into willful creatures intent on destroying both their mates and the sacred institution of the family. (Belton 1994, 198)

A similar argument can be made about Weimar cinema, which also represents a postwar period during which women's roles pose a threat to masculinity. My analysis of film noir and the Weimar street films takes a different slant on the role of women inside and outside the domestic sphere. In film noir, and in the Weimar street film before it, the sacred institution of the family presents a stupefying although safe alternative to urban enticements. In film noir it is not only the men who long to escape from the domestic realm. Women in both types of films appear either as femmes attrapées, virtual slaves in the domestic economy, or as femmes fatales, intent on avoiding the role of indentured servant. The stakes involved in destroying, or avoiding, the familial institution were certainly different for women than for men, but were no less critical. I believe the women in the theater audiences saw and understood the choices that these films delineated as available to women.

For Mitchell Cohen, women are just plain frightening, regardless of their roles in film noir: "The genre's women—les femmes noires—basically came in three types: the girl next door, the deceptive seductress, and the beautiful neurotic. . . . Sociologically, there was a sound [!] basis for this treatment, since it expressed the trepidations of the returning G.I.s who, having been so long without women, had severe doubts about their ability to relate to the mysterious opposite sex" (Cohen 1974, 28). Cohen manages to excise women, and their changing roles, from his explanation of the three types of women in film noir. He does not substantiate his types with specific cinematic examples, but the deceptive seductress and beautiful neurotic might both be categorized as femmes fatales and the girl next door probably functions as a potential femme attrapée. In her essay "How Hollywood Deals with the Deviant Male," Deborah Thomas suggests that "the 'marrying woman,' who sets her sights on the hero to his obvious but unavowed discomfiture," presents a threat equal to that of the femme fatale (Thomas 1992, 68). For Thomas, film noir dramatizes points of male crisis, "such as those between wartime and peace, and bachelorhood and marriage" (68). My appropriation and reinterpretation of the term *femme fatale,* and invention of the term *femme attrapée,* serve as an attempt to disrupt the persistence of vision that insists on male victimhood in both the Weimar street film and film noir. I suggest that existence inside or outside the

domestic sphere was equally threatening for the female characters in film noir, that the men returning from service might present a divisive threat to the women to whom they returned, and
that these fears are also recorded in the anxiety that permeates
film noir.

The Stuff of Dreams
Film Noir and *The Maltese Falcon*

I haven't lived a good life. I've been bad. Worse than you could know.

—Brigid O'Shaughnessy in
The Maltese Falcon (1941)

THE noir mood first appears full-blown in the *Maltese Falcon*, with a femme fatale, Brigid O'Shaughnessy (Mary Astor), and a tough-talking detective, Sam Spade (Humphrey Bogart). Brigid does not quite wrest narrative control from Spade, but does give him a run for his money. Spade and Brigid share the ability to make language work for them; it is precisely Brigid's abilities as a liar that prompt Spade to remark, "You're good. You're very good." Just as *The Street* provides a model for Weimar street films, *The Maltese Falcon*, commonly referred to as the first film noir, provides a paradigm for many noirs to follow. As Thomas Schatz observes, the hard-boiled detective narrative "assumed the viewpoint of the isolated, self-reliant 'private eye,'" who uses "his individual talents and streetwise savvy to survive within a sordid, crime-infested city" (Schatz 1981, 123). The femme fatale adds to the dangers of the crime-infested city, as she does in the Weimar Street film. In the silent world of Weimar cinema, and in the films that appeared soon after the advent of sound, the femme fatale is above all visually seductive. In film noir, she achieves her goals not only through seduction, but also through her verbal acuity. The realm of the home and family, a necessary visual element in Weimar street films, receives only lip service in *The Maltese Falcon*, but returns to the screen in later films noirs.

The 1941 version of *The Maltese Falcon* is John Huston's directorial debut, and the third filmed version of Dashiell Hammett's novel. The previous two versions, *The Maltese Falcon* (1931) directed by Roy del Ruth and *When Satan Met a Lady* (1936) directed by William Dieterle and starring Bette Davis, were not especially successful. Huston's careful set-ups and tight shooting schedule allowed the film to be completed in two months, and kept the budget to $300,000, remarkable even in 1941. Bogart for the first time plays a leading man who is not a gangster or gunslinger, and this paves the way for his popular success in the forties and fifties. Veteran stage actor Sidney Greenstreet, at the age of sixty-one, appears on the silver screen for the first time as the jovial and diabolical Kaspar Gutman. And Walter Huston, the director's father, insisting on a role in his son's first film, appears as the doomed Captain Jacobi. He delivers the falcon to Spade's office, mumbles a few words, and falls dead. *The Maltese Falcon* was nominated for Best Picture, Best Supporting Actor (Sydney Greenstreet), and Best Original Screenplay. According to William Nolan, "Warners an-nounced that a sequel would soon follow: *The Further Adventures of the Maltese Falcon* to be written and directed by Huston, re-teaming Bogart, Astor, Greenstreet and Lorre" (Nolan 1965, 42).[1]

The male characters—the hard-boiled Spade, the obese and urbane Gutman, the well-dressed, gardenia-perfumed Cairo (Peter Lorre), and gun-toting Wilmer (Elisha Cook)—spring to mind the instant one thinks of *The Maltese Falcon*. The female characters are also artfully drawn, although with less attention to detail. One of the female roles, that of Spade's secretary Effi (Lee Patrick), harks back to the girl Fridays in films of the 1930s. Effi might also be a precursor to those occasional women in film noir who actively pursue their goals and desires and live to tell of it, such as Vivian (Lauren Bacall) in *The Big Sleep* (1946) and Ann (Anne Shirley) in *Murder, My Sweet* (1944). Although we never see Effi's home, she talks of living with her mother. As I mentioned earlier, home and family receive only lip service in *The Maltese Falcon,* but in Effi's case the spectator is inclined to believe in the existence of her mother in the diegesis of the film. Their relationship stands in marked contrast to the imagined or pseudofamilial relationships of the other female characters in *The Maltese Falcon.* Effi is at once desexualized and marked as trustworthy by her proximity with her mother, although even the honorable Effi lies to her mother when necessary.

Another female character, Iva (Gladys George), seems submerged in a web of deceit. Although married to Spade's partner, Archer, Iva is no femme attrapée. She is having an affair with Spade, and appears to lead the life of a femme fatale in some other narrative, which leaves her with just a little time to spy on Spade, or to drop in on him to accuse him of killing her husband or to insist he come visit her. As Effi tells Spade, Iva "hadn't been home many minutes, when I arrived to break the news [of her husband's death] at three o'clock this morning. . . . Her clothes were on a chair. . . . Her slip, on top, was still warm" (Anobile 1974, 38–39). Iva's activities remain shrouded in mystery, but the narrative of the *Maltese Falcon* does provide enough information to confirm a lack of devotion in her marriage. Early in the film Archer (Jerome Cowan), Spade's partner and Iva's husband, appears lecherously willing to take the case of an attractive female client. Archer next appears on screen just long enough to be shot by an unknown assailant, and provides Iva with the opportunity to dress in black and play the role of grieving widow. Archer appears as a man willing to cheat on his wife and his wife turns out to be equally willing to cheat on him. Iva looks like a femme fatale, but the film eventually reveals Brigid O'Shaughnessy, played by Mary Astor, as the more dangerous woman—one who hides her murderous avariciousness beneath a breathless and innocent exterior.

Mary Astor lived a complicated off-screen life, which included a "love affair with John Barrymore, four marriages, alcoholism, and attempted suicide," as well as a custody battle over her daughter in 1936 in which her "personal diary was introduced in court, listing indiscretions that embarrassed many in the film community" (Katz 1994, 57). The subject of "the most publicized scandal of the thirties," Mary Astor's personal problems negatively affected her acting career, at least until 1941, when she won a best supporting actress Academy Award for *The Great Lie,* starring Bette Davis, and appeared in the *Maltese Falcon* (57). The historically contiguous spectators, male or female, knew they could believe Mary Astor when she insisted she had been bad. Early in the *Maltese Falcon* the character calls herself Miss Wonderly and masquerades as a concerned sibling interested in hiring detective Spade and his partner Archer to find her nonexistent sister before their make-believe parents return home from Honolulu. She lies sincerely, locating herself in a false familial setting and projecting intense filial concern in order to conceal her duplicitous aims. Her real goal is the elimination of her male partner, with whom she is unwilling to share the Maltese falcon, a jewel-encrusted bird covered with lead. Nolan asserts that Huston had Mary Astor "run around the set several times before she appeared to give her a certain nervous, quick-breathing appeal" (Nolan 1965, 41). In her autobiography, Astor admits she "hyper-ventilated before going into most of the scenes" (Astor 1971, 160). Huston describes Astor's characterization of Brigid: "her voice hesitant, tremulous and pleading, her eyes full of candor. She was the enchanting murderess to my idea of perfection" (Huston 1980, 79). Brigid uses her apparent innocence and need for protection, as well as her ability as a liar and her sexuality, to maneuver through the criminal world she inhabits.

Frank Krutnik finds Brigid less eroticized than other femmes fatales and insists Spade "is never in any real danger of being overwhelmed by his desire for the erotic woman. Brigid never poses any real threat to his rationality, his control, or his phallic self-containment" (Krutnik 1991, 96). True, she does not wear the tight-fitting, low-cut gowns of Rita Hayworth in *Gilda* (1946), or Lizabeth Scott in *Dead Reckoning* (1947). She does not work as a model or nightclub singer, devices that often provide a diegetic excuse for an eroticized display of the female body.[2] Yet Brigid presents a danger to Spade precisely because she does not seem to display herself. In her discussion of Hammett's novel, Jasmine Yong Hall points out that "Brigid's most impressive skill . . . is not her sexual allure; her abilities as a storyteller are far more impressive" (J. Y. Hall 1990, 112). The film version of the *Maltese Falcon* maintains the novel's characterization of Brigid as a dazzling liar, as well as Spade's appreciation of her talents. For James Maxfield, "Spade is attracted to Brigid . . . because she is a dark mirror image of himself" (Maxfield 1996, 23). Hall asserts that Spade's admiration stems from his own "ability to construct a story quickly" (J. Y. Hall 1990, 112). In the course of the film Spade lies glibly to Iva, to Brigid, and even to the police. If she had not murdered Spade's partner, Brigid might have survived the noir narrative of the *Maltese Falcon*, as "strong women . . . who achieve something of a parity with the men they fall for" occasionally do (Hirsch 1981, 21).

Brigid uses any means necessary to achieve her goals: lying, sexual favors, murder . . . even kicking. In one sequence, Brigid spars with another criminal, Cairo, on the trail of the valuable falcon, suggesting he used his sexuality to "get around" a boy in Istanbul. Cairo responds by implying Brigid had no luck in seducing the same boy. Brigid wastes no time, proceeding to slap and then kick Cairo.[3] The spectator is left to wonder if she reacts so vehemently because Cairo suggests she would attempt such a seduction or because her attempt was unsuccessful.

Despite Krutnik's critical discounting of Brigid's erotic power and Cairo's diegetic maligning of it, the character has obviously been adroit in enlisting the aid of various men throughout her criminal career, and she counts on exerting that power over Spade. In one of the final sequences of the film, Spade reveals that he knows Brigid killed his partner, Archer, and tells her he is resolved to "send her over" despite his feelings for her. Spade tells Brigid, "chances are you'll get off with life. That means if you're a good girl, you'll be out in twenty years. I'll be waiting for you. If they hang you, I'll always remember you." Maxfield notes, "It is not Brigid herself who threatens Spade so much as it [is] his 'love' for her [sic]" (1996, 23). In *Hollywood's Dark Cinema*, R. Barton Palmer incorrectly describes the end of *The Maltese Falcon*, suggesting Spade unfairly singles out Brigid to take the fall: "Only the duplicitous woman is made to bear the legal costs of their misadventures, which include three murders. She is handed over to the police by her erstwhile lover, the detective Sam Spade . . . who gives up the woman he loves because he prefers looking out for himself" (Palmer 1994, 73). In fact, Spade arranges with the police for the arrest of all the nefarious characters that populate *The Maltese Falcon*, and the police tell Spade they "got 'em all." Spade does hand Brigid over to the police. The final scene of the film provides a close-up of Brigid in the elevator with a police officer, the shadow of the bars of the elevator gate directly across her face (fig. 17). Alain Silver claims that with "Spade, the viewer is getting a thrill out of sending Brigid over" (Silver and Ward 1992, 182). But the reverse-shot of Spade, also in close-up, does not present a gloating, triumphant visage but rather a face torn by doubt and resignation (fig. 18). As the frosted-glass inner door of the elevator obscures Brigid from Spade's and the spectator's view, he descends the staircase holding the fake falcon, "the stuff that dreams are made of."

In the *Maltese Falcon* the realm of the home and family has also been reduced to the stuff that dreams are made of, and the femme fatale does her part to reveal the diaphanous quality of those dreams. The Weimar film *The Street* and *The Maltese Falcon* feature a male protagonist. In *The Street*, he leaves his home and wife for the pleasures and distractions of the city and the femme fatale is included in the list of those distractions. He eventually returns home resigned to his safe if dull home life. In *The Maltese Falcon* the male protagonist makes his living on the streets. His meeting with the femme fatale is not just one of a series of dangerous distractions but the driving force of the film's narrative. Unlike her counterpart in *The Street*, the femme fatale in *The Maltese Falcon* appears as mistress of her own fate. She attempts, like the male criminal characters in the film, to insure that the outcome of the search for unimaginable

Figures 17–18. The narrative and visual containment of the femme fatale . . . and the doubt and resignation of the male protagonist (*The Maltese Falcon*, 1941)

prosperity embodied in the falcon winds up in her favor. Both femmes fatales pay for their crimes and wind up contained by prison bars. The Weimar street film developed from a cycle specifically concerned with male identity or class into one that allowed female identity equal or greater emphasis. Even if the narrative insists on a recontainment of female desire in the final reel, its expression remains central to the texts. Film noir takes up where the Weimar cycle leaves off. In the early Weimar crime melodrama, the domestic sphere associated with the femme attrapée seems at once dull and yet safely sealed off from the dangers of the street, often embodied by the femme fatale. But the boundaries between the home and the urban milieu become more permeable; the wife ventures onto the street, and the femme fatale visits the home. In film noir, the distinction between the two realms becomes even more blurred.

CHAPTER 9

Why Do You Have To Murder People?

The Femme Fatale and Femme Attrapée in *Gun Crazy*

> Two people dead just so we can live without working.
> Why? Why did you do it? Why do you have to murder
> people? Why can't you let them live?
> —Bart Tare to Annie Laurie Starr
> in *Gun Crazy*

LIKE the Weimar street film *Variety*, the 1950 film *Gun Crazy*, directed by Joseph H. Lewis, features a circus milieu.[1] Like *Variety*, *Gun Crazy* provides the spectator with the two versions of femininity I have identified as paradigmatic for many street films and films noirs, a femme attrapée and a femme fatale. In *Gun Crazy*, the femme fatale also trades up, exchanging one lover for another who seems to offer more opportunities for her advancement. Like *Variety*, the narrative of *Gun Crazy* tells the tale of the male protagonist. Yet, as in many films noirs, the femme fatale in *Gun Crazy* drives the narrative and her agency energizes the film—so much so that her eventual demise engenders a certain ambivalence. I have suggested that as the Weimar street film developed, the female characters, especially the femmes fatales, began to take visual and narrative precedence over the male protagonists. In film noir this trend continues. Although film noir is traditionally defined as a masculine form, its more interesting story is often a feminine scenario.

Toward the end of the film, Bart Tare, the male protagonist

in *Gun Crazy* (originally released as *Deadly Is the Female*), poses the above questions to his female companion, Annie Laurie Starr. The answers I propose in the course of this discussion of *Gun Crazy* become logical only when attention shifts from the male protagonist to the representations of women in the film. *Gun Crazy* features a gun-toting femme fatale who shoots to kill—a woman whose vitality initially proves irresistible to the male protagonist and the film spectator, regardless of gender.[2] This type of female character, "active, adventurous and driven by sexual desire," constitutes a large part of the visual and narrative enticements offered by film noir (Cowie 1993, 135). In *Gun Crazy*, the text of the femme fatale is contrasted with a barely concealed subtext—one of female domestic drudgery as the only option available to the ideologically acceptable "woman" on the screen, the woman I identify as a femme attrapée.

Before discussing the female characters in *Gun Crazy*, I want to show how the film is constructed as a masculine scenario. In *The Dark Side of the Screen*, Foster Hirsch describes the film as "the case history of a man whose gun fixation dates from his childhood" (Hirsch 1981, 195). Certainly the first twelve minutes unfold as a case history. The first sequence in the film takes place in a typical haunt of film noir—a city street at night in pouring rain, with a hotel sign flashing in the background. In a continuous shot, the camera dollies back, revealing that it watches from inside a shop window. A boy comes around the corner; he gazes longingly into the window at the guns displayed and then he breaks the window with a rock and steals a gun. As he runs away he trips and the gun slides across the wet pavement to land at the feet of the local sheriff.

The next sequence of the film opens with Ruby (Anabell Shaw), the sister of the young criminal and a femme attrapée, explaining to a judge that her brother Bart has always loved guns, but that he would never kill anything. A flashback shows the young Bart stricken with remorse after shooting a chick in a farmyard, verifying Ruby's view of Bart. It appears that Bart and Ruby are orphaned, and that Ruby has had the responsibility of raising her brother. A series of other witnesses, each with a flashback bridged by a voice-over, tell the judge about Bart's relationship to firearms. Often used as part of an investigative structure in film noir, the flashbacks and voice-over narrations investigate Bart, and his obsession with guns. His boyhood friends, Clyde and Dave, also insist he could never kill anything, and the flashback reveals he would not shoot a mountain lion, although he was more than capable of making the shot. The movie reviewer for *Newsweek* attributes Bart's inability to kill to biological determinism, suggesting that "not being a female, he can't bring himself to use his talent on either human beings or small animals" ("Deadly" 1950, 70). Ruby steps up again as the final witness in Bart's behalf, saying that she is to be married, and that her future husband says it is all right to have Bart live with them, that Bart "needs a man around the house." But the judge tells Ruby that "adjusting to marriage is a job all in itself, without assuming handicaps right at the start," and sends Bart off to reform school.

Gun Crazy tells Bart's story. But Ruby's story is also told,

Figure 19. Ruby—a femme attrapée (*Gun Crazy*, 1953)

however obliquely, and the story of "the famous, the danger-ous, [and] the beautiful" Annie Laurie Starr (Peggy Cummins), the femme fatale who lures Bart into a life of crime, becomes understandable only when read alongside Ruby's and Bart's tale. As I mention earlier, Ruby embodies the antithesis of the femme fatale, the femme attrapée (fig. 19). A brief sequence, lasting less than a minute of screen time, shows how Ruby's life has changed since her marriage. Bart, now an adult, has appar-ently returned home from a stint in the army. The sound of a telephone ringing provides a sound bridge as the shot fades into a tight close-up of a telephone. The next shot shows Ruby, looking frazzled and exhausted, hurrying to answer the phone as she dries her hands. Two young children sit eating at the kitchen table. Ruby's harried expression conveys weariness, al-though when she hears it is Bart calling she brightens slightly. She tells him the kids are wonderful, and to come on over. She then hangs up the phone and tells the children their uncle Bart has come home. Bart's visit with Ruby and the children remains part of the story, but not part of the plot of *Gun Crazy*, further devaluing their importance to him.[3] Since the film spectator does not see him fondly greeting his sister and embracing his niece and nephew, Bart's later assertion that it feels "pretty im-portant" to be an uncle remains unsubstantiated by the visual information provided by the film. Ruby, a femme attrapée, does appear as the antithesis of Annie Laurie Starr (called Laurie), the femme fatale of *Gun Crazy*. While Laurie strides across stage, the camera barely able to contain her gestures, Ruby is trapped either by the tight framing of the shot, or by the do-mestic clutter of the kitchen. She is not portrayed as passive or static, so much as limited and restrained by her environment, and if she seems dull, it might be due to her visible exhaustion. A home might offer an idyllic safe haven for a man, but Ruby has traded her job as mother and sister to Bart for an even more exhausting position. Avoiding the apparent confinement of Ruby's life is at least part of what drives Laurie and perhaps Bart as well.

Ruby and Bart's boyhood friends appear to live orderly and

productive lives in small-town America, at least until a traveling show brings Laurie to town. In *Postmodernist Fiction*, Brian McHale notes that "traveling shows frequently function in postmodernist fantastic texts as agents of disruption, vehicles for insinuating the supernatural or paranormal into 'normal' reality" (McHale 1987, 174). These cinematic texts strive for a certain realism, and the circus and traveling show allow the introduction of scandalous and criminal behavior into the narratives. In the carnival milieu of the Weimar text *Variety*, the dangers and pleasures of the urban landscape appear condensed and intensified by the spectacular extravagance of the huge carnival in the Berlin Wintergarten, as well as by the performers themselves. The film audience enjoys the show with its dancing dwarfs, acrobats, exotic dancers, and comedians. In *Variety* the narrative of love betrayed occasionally recedes in favor of the visual enticements of unusual and wondrous spectacle—a spectacle whose participants are themselves agents of disruption. The carnival serves a dual function in *Variety*; it provides a context for the presentation of exciting and enticing circus acts to the film spectator, and it represents a moral and social environment in which love affairs and murder can unfold. In *Gun Crazy* the traveling show transports the danger and allure of the urban environment into a rural one. The carnival provides a vehicle for the femme fatale's entrance into town, and she gets top billing. The film audience gets only a momentary glimpse of the other spectacles offered by the traveling show, a behind-the-scenes dolly shot showing various barkers and exotic dancing girls, before being transported into the tent to meet the femme fatale. Unlike *Variety*, *Gun Crazy* cuts to the chase. In film noir, the femme fatale becomes the dominant focus—of the camera, the male protagonist, and the film audience.

Laurie, a sharpshooter, takes center stage from the moment she is introduced during her circus act as "so appealing, so dangerous, so lovely to look at." For Jim Kitses, Laurie's entrance compares favorably with the "most stunning entrances in all of cinema," "her charming and spirited debut . . . a fair bid for attention, a triumphant seizing of the stage" (Kitses 1996, 27). In a low-angle continuous shot Laurie strides into the frame, shooting two guns over her head, stopping when she fills the frame in a medium close-up. She appears to size up someone in the carnival tent, or the diegetic audience (and by implication, the audience in the theater). Suddenly, she appears to look specifically at someone, and an eyeline match shows Bart in medium close-up, leaning forward and smiling.[4] In a shot/reverse shot sequence (literally), a cut takes us back to Laurie, who takes aim and fires her gun, loaded with blanks, directly at Bart (fig. 20). A cut to Bart shows him flinch and then laugh outright. The sequence ends with a cut to a medium close-up of Laurie, her face obscured by the foregrounded gun she has pointed directly at the camera. Usually, in a shot/reverse shot pattern, an establishing shot "delineates the overall space" included in the sequence (Bordwell and Thompson 1993, 265). In the series of shots described above, the spectator never sees

Figure 20. "So appealing, so dangerous, so lovely to look at." Annie Laurie Starr—a femme fatale (*Gun Crazy*, 1951)

an orienting establishing shot. The organization of space remains graphically discontinuous. While the shot/reverse shot pattern leads us to believe Bart is the object of Laurie's gaze, a degree of doubt remains. The spectator in the cinema might also have been in her gun sight. In either case, Laurie actively looks at what interests her.

The psychoanalytic implications of the woman with the gun are difficult to avoid, and most critics of *Gun Crazy* do not bother to try. For Frank Krutnik, she is a "woman who has usurped the male right" to the possession of the weapon/power (Krutnik 1991, 221). According to Krutnik, "Bart's attraction to Laurie seems to be motivated by his desire to find someone who can embody the paternal position of power and authority and thus allow him to find his place" (221). Hirsch also finds Bart's male identity unstable, stating that "the character's fascination with guns, obviously, is a compensation for his lack of manliness" (Hirsch 1981, 195). Hirsch claims Bart is played by "an appropriately weak actor" (195), John Dall, who incidentally also starred as the perverse murderer in Alfred Hitchcock's *Rope* (1948). Whether Hirsch means John Dall played the character of Bart as though he were weak, or he found the quality of Dall's acting poor, the implications of both Krutnik's and Hirsch's remarks seems clear—Bart is not manly enough, and therefore he succumbs to Laurie. Stanley Kauffmann, commenting on *Gun Crazy* (upon its release on video in 1991), agrees with Krutnik and Hirsch. According to Kauffmann, the film "tries to imply strong sexual themes: the pistol as phallus, [Laurie] as sexually aroused by robbing and killing, [Bart] a skilled sharpshooter who is seduced into using his talent in crime (a woman teaches him the complete use of his phallus)" (Kauffmann 1991, 26). The psychoanalytic approach often reduces narratives to the same basic set of oedipal, and usually masculine, scenarios, eliminating the possibility that a film might contain some other scenario, namely, a feminine one.

Not surprisingly, Laurie's actions and motivations remain a mystery to Hirsch: "We have no idea as to how the woman got as maniacal as she is. Fearless, taunting, utterly without moral scruples, she goads the passive hero into a cycle of robberies and shootings, her expertise with guns a sign of her essential and unstoppable violence" (Hirsch 1981, 195). Likewise, the 1950 *Newsweek* reviewer claims the film does not explain "[h]ow [Laurie] got to be the gun-moll type in the first place," or "why [Bart] is so willing to marry a patently bad egg like [Laurie] and fall in with her larcenous schemes" ("Deadly" 1950, 70). Kitses takes a more sympathetic view of Laurie, making the intriguing suggestion that her violent aggression might be compensation for a disabling fear of physical violation. He sees "her mystery as a sign of humanity, rather than tired proof of her spidery qualities" (Kitses 1996, 62). Perhaps the explanation for Laurie's lawlessness remains ambiguous because of the text's emphasis on Bart and his motivations. But the reason Bart falls in with Laurie's schemes is sex, and the film makes this obvious, despite the production code of the time, which insisted that "excessive and lustful kissing, lustful embraces, suggestive postures and gestures" were not to be shown (Leff and Simmons 1990, 285). Laurie tells Bart she will leave him and begin a life of crime on her own if he will not join her in a robbery. She then gets horizontal and suggests that she and Bart "finish things like [they] began them—on the level," as she entices him to join her on the bed.[5] Needless to say, Bart does join her on the bed, and falls in with her larcenous schemes.

Laurie seduces Bart into a life of crime. But Bart's obsession with guns, and his willingness to break the law to satisfy his desire, has much to do with his willingness to be seduced. When Bart returns from the army and talks with his boyhood friends about the experience, he claims he found the army dull. I believe Bart would find a forty-dollar-a week job with Remington equally dull, and Laurie provides him with a ticket out of a life he can hardly stand. Both Laurie and Bart appear to come from roughly the same social class (although Laurie is British) and to have a similar lust for a life beyond the small-town milieu, which they might occupy if they did not wind up like Bonnie and Clyde in *Gun Crazy*. Laurie explains why she will not settle for the "normal" life Bart suggests for them, saying it is "too slow" for her. She claims she wants "to do a little living." Laurie "doesn't want to be afraid of life or anything else," and as the narrative goes on to show, guns help her keep this fear at bay. According to Krutnik, "*Gun Crazy* gives violent and vicarious expression to desires which are manifestly and inherently 'criminal'" (Krutnik 1991, 226). I do not dispute the manifest criminality of Laurie, and, thanks to Laurie's goading, of Bart. Although *Gun Crazy* presents Laurie as dangerous and lawless, a certain ambiguity infuses the film's presentation of the alternatives available to her, and by extension, to the female spectator.

Laurie's choices must be read alongside Ruby's existence— the apparently dreary life of a femme attrapée. Ruby's husband (or husband-to-be) only appears on the screen for an instant, during the courtroom scene. Ruby appears a virtual domestic slave, forever trapped in the kitchen or on the porch of the family home, or finally, locked off-screen in the garage with her children by Laurie—the femme attrapée imprisoned by the femme fatale.[6] As Harvey notes, "[i]n the free labor that it requires the mother to perform in raising the child, the family serves to legitimate a whole series of practices that oppress women" (Harvey 1978, 24). *Gun Crazy* does not hide these repressive relationships beneath a veneer of domestic bliss. Ruby is always at home, always exhausted, and always the sole caregiver for an ever-increasing brood of children. For Kitses, the relationship between Ruby and Laurie is "insistently generic," with "Ruby in her white blouse and checked apron, cooking in the service of her family, the suspicious Laurie leaning casually against a cupboard in her black dress, doing her nails, staring" (Kitses 1996, 58). But Kitses goes on to make the same observations I have made about Ruby, suggesting that Ruby's enmity toward Laurie might "be fuelled by bitterness at her [Ruby's] life's mockery of the period's ideal dream home and family, her life of drudgery while hubby is off on a business trip" (59). Even the visual texture of the film refuses to glorify the domestic realm. Gray tones dominate in the kitchen, and the porch of the family home seems like an extension of the gray clutter that surrounds her. Twenty-five years after *Variety*, the wife's position in society seems much the same.

Like Ruby's husband, Bart's boyhood friends are equally detached from their spouses, and occupy the public spheres of the newspaper office or police station. Although each pays lip service to home and family, the visual information provided by the film suggests the public is the realm of men, and the private the less-valued realm of women, and the two seldom meet. Ruby, in a sense, stands in for the imaginary spectator, the woman positioned by patriarchal ideology. Although Ruby does not rebel, Laurie does. Bart and Laurie's *amour fou*, their intense connection to one another and their mutual attraction to the excitement of criminality, presents a seductive alternative to Ruby's life.

One of the two people Laurie kills in the course of the film is her superior at a meat-packing plant where she and Bart have taken jobs while planning their final holdup. Laurie ostensibly shoots a woman, Miss Sifert (Anne O'Neal), for pulling the burglar alarm during the holdup. But just before the holdup, Miss Sifert challenges Laurie about her dress, or lack thereof: "May I ask why you're wearing slacks?" Laurie demurely apologizes, saying her dry cleaning had not come back. Her supervisor responds disapprovingly: "I'll expect you tomorrow in a skirt." The sequence goes on to make it quite clear that Laurie shoots Miss Sifert as she pulls the burglar alarm, but one cannot help wondering if Laurie would have shot so accurately if Miss Sifert had not just asserted her authority over Laurie, insisting Laurie dress the part of a woman Laurie would rather die than play.[7] In his essay on American film noir, James Naremore notes that the story "allows a woman to wear the pants and act as the aggressive partner," and that early French critics Borde and Chaumeton call *Gun Crazy* a film noir of "exemplary beauty" (Naremore 1995, 12).

At least part of that beauty stems from the sight of Laurie fighting her battle. Why does Laurie have to murder people just so she and Bart can live without working? She does it to avoid the lot of women like Ruby, to insist that her relationship with Bart be a passionate adventure, and to defy at every instance a society that must, and eventually does, contain her. For Laurie, it is a case of kill or be killed. Dana Polan would seem to concur with my assessment of why Laurie kills: "[i]t is easy at the end of a film like *Gun Crazy* to feel emotionally ambivalent about the ending's sense: is it good or not that the bland forces of small-town America . . . have won out over all the excessive energy of a woman like Laurie?" (Polan 1986, 204). I believe the film is structured around this emotional ambivalence, an ambivalence that must have been especially relevant for women in the theater audience. Ruby, the ideologically "good" woman and a femme attrapée, lives a static, gray, exhausted existence and is committed to maintaining the status quo. Laurie, in her brief assumption of the role of working woman, finds herself subject to the same constrictions that plague women in the domestic realm. She can only perform tasks delineated as woman's work and must dress the part as well. Laurie shoots her way out of the bind of acceptable behavior, and, as usual for femmes fatales, pays with her life. As spectators, especially of Hollywood narratives of the forties and fifties, we know Laurie must and will be contained in the final reel, just as the psychoanalytic analysis of Bart's story ensures his eventual submission to the law—he realizes she must be killed as well.[8] Bart shoots Laurie, and is then shot to death by the police. But it is Laurie's adamant refusal to be contained by anything less than a bullet through the heart that makes *Gun Crazy* a powerful feminine scenario, and a film noir feast for a female spectator.

Film Noir Traps All Femmes
All Women Are Femmes Fatales
in *The Big Heat*

I've been rich and I've been poor. Believe me,
rich is better.
> —Debbie to police detective Dave Bannion
> in *The Big Heat*

HE Big Heat (Fritz Lang, 1953) provides the consummate film noir sequel to the late Weimar street film *Asphalt*. The associated realms of the street and the home in the narrative of *Asphalt* become indistinguishable in *The Big Heat*. Both films provide the viewer with a domestic sphere associated with the male protagonist that seems at once idyllic and humane. But the domestic realm also appears in many other guises in *The Big Heat*, which represents familial life as a sham, as a relationship of convenience, as perverse, and finally as so fragile and threatened that even an icon of domesticity becomes a weapon.[1] Like *Asphalt*, *The Big Heat* features a male police officer and a femme fatale who develops from self-centered to altruistic in the course of the film, until she finally turns against the forces of the street in an act of self-sacrifice. In *The Big Heat*, however, with only minor exceptions all the female characters, including the wife of the male protagonist, end up dead, and none of them die of natural causes. The film boasts a rich assortment of female roles; the femme fatale mentioned above, who finally resolves the issues confronting the male protagonist, a femme fatale with a heart of gold, a femme fatale masquerading as a policeman's grieving widow, a wife who seems to thrive on her home and family life, and a brave elderly woman of the sort rarely seen on screen. I am not interested in the irremediable task of recuperating *The Big Heat* and making it into a feminist text. I do want to closely examine the characterization of women in a film that seems on the surface to suggest that the only good woman is a dead woman, to see if any other reading is possible.

In *The Big Heat* violence and criminality contaminate a small city, controlling elections and the police, as well as threatening familial institutions. The archetypal cast of film noir characters is present, but in keeping with many films noirs of the fifties, they have moved out of the shadowy stairwells and back alleys to occupy well-furnished apartments and luxurious estates. Much of the violence occurs off screen—in the diegesis of the film, no doubt occurring in the old haunts of film noir. Violence and criminality still exist, closer and more threatening than ever, but also more insidious. The boundary between the criminal elements and the rest of society is further blurred in *The Big Heat* by the sparing use of those features that distinguish the visual style of film noir: low-key lighting, off-angle compositions, and night-for-night photography.

Emphasizing the encroaching and surrounding danger to the family unit as well as the perversity of certain domestic relationships, the plot of the film takes the viewer into two false fronts of domesticity before introducing the ideal and threatened Bannion family. The opening sequence of the film introduces a husband (only briefly alive) and a wife already corrupted. Setting the violent tone, the first shot of *The Big Heat* is a close-up of a revolver on a desk. As the camera slowly draws back, a hand grasps the gun, a shot is fired, and a man slumps over the desk. The frame continues to enlarge, revealing a woman coming down the stairs. After a cut to a medium shot of the woman, her face half in shadow, and a huge grandfather clock reading three o'clock, the sequence goes on to show her coldly assessing the suicide of her husband and making a phone call. Bertha Duncan (Jeanette Nolan), from the opening sequence a policeman's widow, exhibits the greed and ambition of the archetypal femme fatale, although her sexuality is de-emphasized. I view her as a femme attrapée resolved, on the suicide death of her philandering husband, to break out of her domestic trap. A later sequence, an interview between Mrs. Duncan and homicide detective Dave Bannion (Glenn Ford), visually underscores her duplicity by beginning with a shot of her at a vanity table, reflected in a three-paned mirror as she makes herself up to play the grieving widow. Bertha Duncan's 3 A.M. phone call takes the camera right into the luxurious bedroom of the second false front of domesticity, the home of crime boss Mike Lagana (Alexander Scourby). No mention is made of a wife, and although Lagana talks about his daughter's parties and dates with a football player, she remains in the story but not in the plot, and never appears on screen. Lagana has adopted a facade of respectability that includes an opulent home complete with a portrait of his now dead mother dominating the living room, but his lack of real contact with his daughter stands in marked contrast to the Bannion family.

Having established Dave Bannion as the detective in charge of the Duncan suicide, the sequence introducing this family begins with a newspaper headline confirming Bertha Duncan's story and then pulls back to reveal Bannion reading the paper in a cozy kitchen. As his blond wife, Katie (Jocelyn Brando),[2] clad in a simple polka-dot dress and checked apron, serves their steak and potatoes, Bannion puts away the paper, opens two beers, and they discuss their daughter Joyce. Katie Bannion stands opposed to the femme fatale characters and resembles a femme attrapée in her total association with this domestic realm. But like Holk's mother in *Asphalt,* Katie's vivacity stands in marked contrast to the bland, overworked wives seen in both the Weimar films *Variety* and *The Street,* as well as to Ruby in *Gun Crazy.* In addition, Katie and Bannion's brief stints of verbal sexual sparring, fairly explicit at a time when censors insisted all bedrooms contain only twin beds, rounds out their relationship. When Katie remarks that their daughter is "angelic all day but at night she's a holy terror," Bannion retorts with a grin that that's the way he usually describes Katie. This familial sequence is shot in classical Hollywood style, with high-key lighting cre-

ating minimal, natural-looking shadows in the homey kitchen/
dining room. But outside the gingham-curtained windows, an
intensely black night looms, and phone calls interrupt the domestic idyll.

The first phone call into this seemingly ideal domestic
sphere rouses Bannion from his steak and potatoes and leads
him to a nightclub where he meets the second femme fatale
of the film narrative, the self-described B-girl Lucy Chapman
(Dorothy Green). Lucy appears on screen in only one sequence. She asserts that she and Duncan, the police officer
who committed suicide in the opening scene, were having an
affair, planning to get married, and that he owned a "summer
place . . . down in Lakeside," suggesting to Bannion that things
are not quite as clear-cut as Bertha Duncan would have him
think. Lucy Chapman does follow through on my redefinition
of the femme fatale—her actions prove more deadly to her
than to anyone else. Her questioning of Duncan's suicide leads
directly to her death. According to a police teletype that flash-
es across the screen, Lucy Chapman was "THROWN FROM A
CAR AFTER BEATING AND TORTURE" later on the same night of
her meeting with Bannion. For Fritz Lang, showing the result of
violence instead of the violence itself engages the spectator's
imagination. According to Lang, "I force the audience to become a collaborator of mine; by *suggesting* something I achieve
a greater impression, a greater involvement than by showing it"
(quoted in Bogdanovich 1967, 86; italics in original).[3] Lucy
does not appear as luminous, dangerous, and duplicitous as the
spectator might expect of a woman working in a nightclub in a
film noir. Instead she seems somewhat older and tired, concerned, and sincere about the suicide of a man she cared about.
Despite her obvious sincerity, Bannion does not conceal his
contempt for Lucy's lifestyle or his skepticism about her story.
According to Colin McArthur's analysis, Bannion's initial hos-
tility toward Lucy "increases his bitterness and sense of guilt"
when he finds out about her torture and murder (McArthur
1992, 58).[4] Lucy arouses Bannion's suspicions about the suicide,

and pays with her life. Katie Bannion will also pay with her life, her only crime being her association with her husband.

When Katie answers an apparently obscene call made by one of Lagana's thugs to threaten Bannion off the Duncan case, Bannion knows his home and family have been threatened. He retaliates by barging into Lagana's house and roughing up his bodyguard. Lagana strikes back and in a car explosion intended to kill Bannion, Katie is killed. Katie ventures out of the domestic realm only to pick up the baby-sitter, a foray that ends in disaster for the whole family. As McArthur notes, "the acts of violence against women in *The Big Heat* are cumulative in their ferocity" (68). With Katie's death, a woman totally removed from the criminal elements (except for her contiguity with her policeman husband) takes the fall. The danger of stepping outside the gingham-curtained kitchen proves deadly. The final sequence in the Bannion bungalow takes place after Katie's death. As workers remove the last of the furniture, Bannion refuses the help and sympathy of a fellow policeman, who accuses Bannion of being on a "hate binge." As he stands alone in the empty room, filled with apparently natural light, the camera moves in for a close-up of Bannion's clenched jaw and teary, determined eyes. The camera then records his exit from the house, remaining inside as he gently closes the door on his idyllic past.

Glenn Ford's role as police detective Dave Bannion in *The Big Heat* bears some resemblance to his portrayal of Johnny, the supposed protagonist of *Gilda* (1946). In his essay in *Women in Film Noir*, Richard Dyer makes a powerful case for the film's portrayal of Gilda/Hayworth as "known and normal" and Johnny/Ford as "unknown and deviant" (Dyer 1980, 98). For Dyer, this is a subversion of two aspects he considers generic to film noir:

> Film noir abounds in colorful representations of decadence, perversion, aberrations etc. Such characters and milieux vividly evoke that which is not normal,

through connotations (including of femininity, homosexuality and art) of that which is not masculine. By
inference the hero, questing his way through these
characters and milieux, is normal and masculine. Sec-
ondly, women in film noir are above all else unknow-
able. It is not so much their evil as their unknowabil-
ity (and attractiveness) that makes them fatal for the
hero. (92)

Watching *Gilda* arouses a sense of discomfort in the spectator.
Cinematic conventions lead one to expect Johnny/Ford to
be truthful as his voice-over guides the spectator through the
investigation of both the villain and Gilda/Hayworth. Yet
Johnny's actions and narration become increasingly misogynist
and sadistic, while Gilda becomes more sympathetic and sincere. As Dyer notes in a later essay about homosexuality in film
noir, "Gilda is far from fatal, and . . . there is something patho-
logical in Johnny's . . . violent response to her" (Dyer 1993, 70).
I see something similar occurring in *The Big Heat*.

Bannion's inflexibility, cruelty, and potential for violence is
constantly contrasted with the flexibility, sympathy, and understanding of a female character. Early in *The Big Heat*, Bannion
expresses his frustration and anger at his superior's inaction
against the mobsters who run the town. Katie, his wife, suggests the man is ready for retirement and may not want to risk
his pension, demonstrating a humanity and sympathy Bannion
seems unable to feel. As I note above, Bannion does not bother
to conceal his seething contempt for Lucy Chapman as she attempts to alert him to Bertha Duncan's dishonesty. Lucy hopes
for a fair shake from Bannion, but he cannot listen to her without sneering and warns her not to try to blackmail Bertha
Duncan. After Katie's murder, when Bannion goes to a junkyard
in search of the explosives expert responsible for the car bomb,
the (male) owner refuses to help despite Bannion's threats, insisting he's "got a wife and kids" to protect too. Bannion storms
off, clenching his fists in anger. A middle-aged woman, Selma
Parker (Edith Evanson), whose obvious presence in the junk-

yard office and desire to speak to him is recorded by the camera but remains invisible to Bannion, offers him help outside in the yard. In a series of shots and reverse-shots through a chain-link fence, Selma defends the junkyard owner as a good man, one willing to hire a woman like Selma (I assume this means elderly, with a cane and a limp). She also provides Bannion with the information he needs to continue his investigation. According to McArthur, the fence "creates the incarceratory imagery in which Selma is 'imprisoned'" (McArthur 1992, 67). But Bannion is imprisoned too "by the dehumanizing hatred and lust for revenge which consume him" (67). Selma appears on screen once again to knock anonymously at the door of the hoodlum responsible for the explosion, identifying him for Bannion. Selma, and Bannion, seem to be banking on the invisibility of older women, as the hoodlum had presumably seen her at the junkyard. My point here is that Bannion remains callous and obsessed in the face of each of these female character's humanity and bravery.[5] And he does not treat Debbie (Gloria Grahame) any better than Lucy Chapman.

Debbie first notices Bannion in the nightclub where he had previously interviewed Lucy. Following a lead, Bannion arrives in time to see Debbie's boyfriend, Vince (Lee Marvin), burn a woman at the bar with a lighted cigarette, a form of cruelty that clearly marks Vince as Lucy Chapman's murderer. Bannion interferes and Vince leaves the bar, leaving Debbie eyeing Bannion appreciatively. Barely audible as diegetic sound in the bar is the song "Put the Blame on Mame." Central to his analysis of *Gilda*, Dyer asserts that the "song points to how men always blame natural disasters on Mame—that is, women. The song states the case against the way film noir characteristically constructs women" (Dyer 1980, 95). The use of "Mame" as background music at this juncture may be little more than an auspicious coincidence for my analysis, but it does point to the ambivalence the film exhibits toward femmes fatales, despite the virulence with which it annihilates most of them, including Debbie.[6]

Debbie pursues Bannion out of the nightclub, onto the

street, and back to his hotel room. Bannion's obsessive desire for revenge is recorded in the texture of the film—instead of a comfortable cottage he now occupies a shadowy hotel room with a bottle of scotch on the dresser. His first guest there is Debbie, the beautiful, sexually aggressive half of the femme fatale equation that fills the space left by the desexualized Mrs. Duncan. Her sexual intentions, which she defines as "research," make her motivation clear, while Bannion hopes to glean information from her about his wife's killers. For the first time Bannion's image is split in a mirrored reflection, accentuating the dual sides of his character, and connecting him visually with other duplicitous characters. In one shot, Debbie and Bannion gaze at each other, visually linked by black shadows, both intent on their own very separate goals. Despite her alluring appearance, Debbie does not reach her goal. She does casually admit to her reasons for staying with Vince, telling Bannion she has been rich and poor, and rich is better—an assertion almost every femme fatale can make.

Debbie, even more that the other femme fatales I have discussed, cannot pass a mirror without being drawn into a narcissistic admiration of herself. In one of the most grippingly violent occasions film noir has to offer, one that does appear on-screen, her beautiful surface is literally burned off. The sequence takes place in a well-lit apartment full of men playing cards (one of them the police commissioner) and underscores the insidious nature of criminality in the film. In the hands of Debbie's jealous lover, Vince, a boiling pot of coffee becomes a weapon.[7] In this noir world, criminals wear expensive clothing and inhabit fancy dwellings, but their cruelty and sadism remain intact and even unchallenged. For McArthur, this is the "culmination of the violent pattern" of acts against women— "the scalding of Debbie's face [is] an act which not only occurs on-screen, but whose gruesome results are later made visible" (McArthur 1992, 68).

Debbie, her face scarred and bandaged, goes to Bannion for protection and reveals to him the name of the hoodlum directly responsible for his wife's death. A scene of pseudodomesticity follows, with Bannion playing the concerned nurse to the disfigured Debbie.[8] Bannion tells Debbie that the death of Bertha Duncan will release the big heat—a letter damning Lagana—but that he was unable to kill her, although he should have (he does come close to choking her to death).[9] Once Bannion has sown this seed in Debbie's mind and left her alone in the hotel room she does the rest, avenging Katie's murder by shooting Bertha Duncan and retaliating for her own ruined visage by throwing coffee in the face of her lover. Debbie does not wait for a man to come to her aid; instead she does her own dirty work. In the process, she sacrifices herself to maintain the integrity of a man who remains, to a certain degree, as insensitive to her as he has been to the other female characters in *The Big Heat*.

In the penultimate sequence of the film, Bannion has conquered his demons and resists the impulse to shoot Vince, instead turning him over to the police. As Debbie dies, shot by Vince, Bannion tells her about his wife and idyllic family life, saying Katie used to dress their daughter up like a princess and that his favorite time of day was when he got home from work and saw his wife looking like someone who just stepped down off a birthday cake. A close-up of Bannion closes the sequence—as he says, "I guess it's that way with all families." As McArthur notes, Bannion goes on with his talking cure even after Debbie dies (McArthur 1992, 77). Practically the only woman surviving the noir narrative of *The Big Heat* exists as an idealized memory of princess girls and wives as beautiful as birthday cake. The visual style of *The Big Heat* accentuates the positive characterization of the institution of family, while simultaneously presenting family life as helpless against the forces of evil surrounding it. The destruction of Bannion's family arouses his own murderous rage, but he lets Debbie do his dirty work for him and then comforts her as she dies for her trouble.

The final sequence shows Bannion not with his surviving daughter attempting to rebuild some sort of familial life, but at work in the police station.[10] As he resumes his role as homicide detective by answering a hit-and-run report, he utters the final line of the film, telling a colleague to keep the coffee hot! As he returns to the city streets that led to his family's destruction, the icon of domesticity has apparently been reined in and returned to its rightful place on the stove. But the final line of *The Big Heat* can also be read as a warning, a pessimistic message true to the noir sensibility. It is not only in the mean city streets but in every place of business, every government office, and even every family that violence and criminality potentially percolate, waiting to erupt.

Enno Patalas sums up the film's treatment of female characters: "They stand between the systems; they seek to mediate or to make the best of the situation for themselves; they choose one side or the other; they are pulverized" (Patalas et al. 1976, 132).[11] *The Big Heat* unambiguously kills off every major female character, and not one of them dies a pretty death. Women are blown up, tortured, burned, and shot. For me, *The Big Heat* clearly illustrates the problem film noir presents to the female spectator. The drive to contain any sort of female agency that exits in the Weimar street films and the films noirs I discuss has become crushing. The female characters are portrayed by the narrative of the film as reasonable, understandable individuals. Bertha Duncan, faced with her philandering husband's suicide, decides to blackmail the gangster who had previously supported her husband's secret liaisons. Not content to rely on a police officer's pension, she attempts to ensure her own financial security and hopes, as she tells Bannion, "the coming years are going to be just fine." The results of her actions are fatal. Katie Bannion loves her husband and speaks her mind; she is blown to smithereens when she ventures out of her home and into the night, despite the domestic nature of her mission. Lucy Chapman dies for having had an affair with a police officer, tortured and murdered in what the county medical examiner says "looks like a sex crime." Debbie consorts with a gangster, attempts to seduce Bannion, avenges herself and the murder of Katie Bannion, and dies in a pool of blood. The male characters, perpetrators of much of the violence and criminality that infect the milieu, including the often cruel and obsessed Bannion, fare much better. For me, film noir's emphatic insistence on the containment of all female desire and energy at the same time as it admits the possibility of female agency is part of the conundrum film noir presents the female spectator. Despite its thematic similarity to film noir, the Weimar street film at least occasionally avoids this conundrum. And, as we shall see, neo-noir will often allow the concept of female agency freer reign. The dust *The Big Heat*'s narrative raises on its way to the final reel leaves the spectator with a positive view of Katie, Lucy, Selma Parker, and Debbie, despite their forced containment. Perhaps Bannion's separation from his daughter increases her chances for survival.

PART FOUR
Pasts And Presents

Reflections
Women and Representation in the Weimar Street Film and Film Noir

N chapter 1 I locate my work in the realm of cultural studies and, because of my use of close textual analysis, in the realm of traditional film studies. While cultural studies admits the possibility of meaning as consumption-led and of an active viewer conscious of the choices appearing on the cinema screens, traditional film studies frequently neglects those possibilities. Instead, much film studies scholarship suggests that each and every film retells a tale of male oedipal desire. Certainly the Weimar street films and films noirs that I discuss fit comfortably into such scenarios, but in each of these texts, other scenarios are enacted as well. My argument with much of film studies stems from the pessimism implicit in reading each story as *his* story. The female spectator seems to have, as Jane Gaines also notes, two positions in this construct—"either as overvalued 'fetishized' star image . . . exhibited and displayed, no more than a sign in a 'patriarchal exchange,' or as audience, but occupying the point of view reserved for the male" (Gaines 1990, 76). While not denying the viability of those positions, I suggest other positions for her as well.

In the Weimar street film I have shown how the female characters eventually take center screen, despite critical readings that persist in describing these texts as representations of unstable male identity. The first femme fatale encountered in *The Street* is a prostitute who does not act of her own volition, but rather appears to do what her pimp tells her. Although she occasionally serves as the object of the camera's and the male protagonist's gaze, the streets themselves serve as the locus of the excitement and allure that will clothe the femmes fatales in later street films and in film noir. The urban realm, at once the province of danger and desire, contrasts with the quotidian existence represented by the wife or mother and the domestic realm. As I have shown, the domestic realm itself represents a trap, not only for the male protagonist, who escapes from it only to return chastised at the end of his adventures, but also for the woman who remains behind. In *The Street*, *Variety*, *M*, and perhaps most explicitly in *Gun Crazy*, the activity and apparent freedom of the femme fatale are measured against the immobility and enslavement of the femme attrapée in the domestic economy.

In *Asphalt* and *The Big Heat* the portrayal of the domestic realm does admit some possibilities of pleasure for the diegetic woman located there, and by extension, for the women in the audience. Feminist critics might view this positive portrayal of domesticity as an ideological trap for the unsuspecting passive female spectator. But I read both these films as offering the female viewer a choice of femininities. Both films admit the potential for female pleasure in the comfortable security of a rewarding family life and in the pursuit of sexual desires. *Asphalt* keeps those possibilities separate, embodying female (and male) sexual satisfaction in the figure of the femme fatale and domestic satisfaction in the figure of the wife/mother. In *The Big Heat* the characterization of Katie Bannion suggests that both female domestic happiness and sexual satisfaction can be found in the home—a bold presumption indeed. Despite, or perhaps because of, the audacity of that presumption, *The Big Heat* eventually eliminates Katie from the narrative altogether. For me, film noir's insistence on the elimination of all forms of female agency becomes one of the major differences between film noir and the Weimar street film.

The noir femmes fatales I discuss in depth—Brigid in *The Maltese Falcon*, Laurie in *Gun Crazy*, and Debbie and Bertha

Duncan in *The Big Heat*—are emphatically contained in the final sequences of those films. Laurie, Debbie, and Bertha are shot to death; Brigid faces life in prison or death by hanging. Of course, these women have engaged in criminal actions—Brigid and Laurie are murderers and thieves and Debbie murders Bertha Duncan to put an end to Bertha's blackmailing activities. But the virulence with which film noir narratives contain these characters far outstrips the suppression of the male criminals. In all three films, the narrative indicates either visually (as in *The Big Heat*), or through dialogue (as in *The Maltese Falcon*), or by implication (as in *Gun Crazy*) that the male criminal(s) will wind up behind bars. In contrast, the spectator actually sees the female characters behind bars, burned, blown up, or shot.

I am not suggesting that the Weimar street film does not also insist on the containment of female agency, but that the emphatic and often violent nature of that containment is less common in the street film. The prostitute in *The Street* suffers the same fate as the pimp; both are taken off to jail. In *Variety* the stairwell visually imprisons Berta Maria as Huller stoically marches off to the authorities to admit his crime. In *Asphalt* Else is led down the hallway of the police station, but her middle-class lover has just embraced her and promised to wait for her. These female characters are reined in, both visually and narratively, but no more so than the male characters, and certainly much less fatally. As Petro's discussion of Weimar texts indicates, the relatively benign treatment of the femmes fatales in the street films I discuss is not always the rule. My point remains that film noir tends to insist more emphatically and violently on the cancellation of female agency than does the Weimar street film. In the street film, the identificatory allure of the femme fatale remains a viable possibility. In film noir, the pleasures of watching an active woman pursue her financial and sexual goals must be measured against the certainty of her demise.

Yet even the certainty of her demise is not without ambiguity. In her essay on the maternal melodrama, Linda Williams suggests the female spectator "reads" the ambiguity of her own position under patriarchy through her identification with female characters on screen. Discussing the eventual victimization of the female hero in melodrama, Williams notes: "Rather than raging against a fate that the audience has learned to accept, the female hero often accepts a fate that the audience at least partially questions. . . . The . . . female spectator . . . criticises the price of transcendent 'eradication' which the victim-hero must pay. . . . the 'lesson' for female audiences is certainly not to become similarly eradicated themselves" (Williams 1987, 320). Although Williams makes her argument about maternal melodramas, it is equally illuminating for films noirs. The eradication of the femmes fatales, and often other female characters in film noir, comes not in the form of self-sacrifice but through the complete containment of imprisonment or death. I have suggested that female spectators can enjoy the story of an active female character and resist the necessity of her containment, and that such resistance is actually implicit in the structure of many film noir narratives and in the portrayal of female characters.

When I began this study, I hoped to demonstrate that both the Weimar street film and film noir provided opportunities for the female spectator—in same-sex erotic and identificatory desire, and in heterosexual desire. All the films in this study provide opportunities for same-sex erotic and identificatory pleasure for the female spectator in the figure of the femme fatale. I do not deny that the femme fatale might encourage the female spectator to construct herself as an image of male desire. But I agree with Jackie Stacey that the assumption of such an image might in itself be a form of rebellion against other forms of femininity, namely against the image represented by the femme attrapée in many of the texts I discuss. The femme fatale does not only supply the female spectator with an opportunity for masochistic identification; the femme fatale also provides the possibility of agency and of escape from the domestic realm. I agree with Judith Mayne that the cinema provides a place to act out desires other than strictly heterosexual ones—and in this light the femme fatale functions as an object of desire for both the male and female spectator. But how do the street film and film noir address heterosexual female desire?

The Weimar street film admits heterosexual female desire and experience as possibilities through a definite address to the female spectator; film noir does not make the same address. As I have shown, the Weimar film *Variety* explicitly offers the female spectator, both diegetic and extradiegetic, a choice of masculinities in the form of the two male protagonists, Huller and Artinelli. The text likewise suggests that the bored husband so frequently featured in the street film has a female counterpart, a wife fed up with her dull spouse. In *Asphalt* the handsome young police officer drowsing on his bed becomes the object of the camera's, and by extension, the female spectator's gaze, in a sequence that specifically addresses the heterosexual female viewer—at the expense of the heterosexual male spectator. The films noirs I discuss open up no similar opportunities for the female spectator. Although I have suggested that Laurie, the femme fatale in *Gun Crazy*, must be read alongside Ruby, the femme attrapée, the text itself does not present that juxtaposition as explicit. Most first-time viewers would not notice the exhausted Ruby any more than earlier critics of the film do. My point here is that the Weimar street films I discuss actually appeal to the female spectator specifically, addressing her experiences and desires. While film noir also provides pleasures for the female spectator, she is not addressed explicitly.

I suspect that the reasons why Weimar cinema makes an explicit address to the female audience while film noir neglects to do so, and the reasons why the Weimar street film does not deal with the containment of female agency as violently as does film noir, are related. Both film noir and the Weimar street films respond to a series of postwar developments in the twentieth century: urbanization, alienation, and the increased presence of women in the public sphere. Although I problematized the gains made by women in the Weimar years, perhaps the relative liberalism of the time enabled a more humane response to female agency than did the conservatism of the 1940s and 1950s in the United States. That liberalism seems to have also allowed for a conception of an audience that contained both male and female spectators, and included an appeal to both. It certainly makes economic sense to invite the female spectator into the world of a film narrative. As I mentioned, in the United States, the threat embodied by the woman in the public sphere was neatly contained, both socially and cinematically, in texts that required the female characters to accept responsibility for the social disruptions of the postwar period. If the femme fatale was the only female character who refused responsibility, and insistently continued the quest to fulfill her own desires, per-haps it should not surprise spectators to see that she must die.

In both Weimar Germany and in the United States, women were in movie audiences and made decisions about which films to see. In my view, the activity of the femmes fatales made these films attractive to many female spectators. In the Weimar street film, the heterosexual female spectator was also offered pleasures designed to appeal to her desires. The violent recon-tainment of female agency in the final reel of the noir films was part of the price the spectator paid for her pleasures. In the Weimar street film, the psychic costs were not quite as high.

Noir Now

Retro-Noir, German Neo-Noir, U.S. Neo-Noir

AS I mentioned in the introduction, film noir has lately become ubiquitous, not only in the cinema, but in popular culture as well. James Naremore suggests that "film noir belongs to the history of ideas as much as to the history of cinema; it has less to do with a group of artifacts than with a discourse—a loose, evolving system of arguments and readings, helping shape commercial strategies and aesthetic ideologies" (Naremore 1995, 14). Certainly many commercial strategies and aesthetic ideologies in the late 1990s are informed by film noir. Recently the Seattle Museum of Art hosted a film noir poster show, and the grocery stores in Utah carry a perfume called *Noir Exclamation!* One only has to glance at the *New York Times* movie reviews to see that the noir aesthetic is still enticing to film spectators and filmmakers alike. The 1994 film *Pulp Fiction*, directed by Quentin Tarantino, makes obvious reference to film noir not only in the title of the film but also in its complicated narrative structure. The briefcase in *Pulp Fiction*, with its mysterious, glowing contents, evokes "the great whatsit," a case containing radioactive material that provides the final, apocalyptic explosion in the classic late noir *Kiss Me Deadly* (1955). *Jackie Brown* (1997), also directed by Tarantino, stars Pam Grier of blaxploitation fame as a wily and beautiful femme fatale who escapes with the money and the car at the end of the film. Many films of the 1970s—such as *Klute* (1971), *Chinatown* (1974), *The Long Goodbye* (1973), *Taxi Driver* (1976)—also explore noir themes of alienation, perversity, and survival in an urban environment. According to John Belton, in *Chinatown* and *The Long Goodbye* the stylistic elements of film noir "trigger a conventional acknowledgment on the part of viewers who identify that look with films of the late 1940s" (Belton 1994, 192). A style that was intended to disorient becomes in retro- and neo-noir a look that orients the viewer. Silver and Ward identify the post-1950s films, especially those from the late seventies to the present, as neo-noir and insist the productions that "recreate the noir mood, whether in remakes or new narratives, have been undertaken by filmmakers cognizant of a heritage and intent on placing their own interpretation on it" (Silver and Ward 1992, 398).[1] I agree, and use the term *neo-noir* to describe texts that refer back to visual or narrative aspects of the noir of the forties and fifties but that are set in the present—films such as *Twilight* (1998), *Palmetto* (1998), and *The Last Seduction* (1994). I use *retro-noir* to describe films set in the forties or fifties, the time when films noirs were actually being made. *L.A. Confidential* (1997), *Mulholland Falls* (1996), and *Devil in a Blue Dress* (1995) are examples of retro-noir. Three films, a U.S. retro-noir, a German neo-noir, and a U.S. neo-noir, exemplify some of the more recent concerns of noir. While those concerns touch on gender, other issues also surface.

U.S. Retro-Noir: Race and Gender in
Devil in a Blue Dress

On the face of it, race does not seem to have been a dominant focus in film noir. Eric Lott in "The Whiteness of Film Noir" asserts these films actually respond to the threat of racial unrest: "film noir is . . . a sort of whiteface dream-work of social anxieties with explicitly racial sources, condensed on film into the criminal undertakings of abjected whites" (Lott 1997, 551). Lott makes a strong case for "white darkness in noir," and also sees that dark otherness reflected in female characters, specifically the femmes fatales (545). But what, if anything, do neo-noirs and retro-noirs have to say about race? In *Cinema and Modernity*, John Orr makes a case for *Bird* (1988) as a noir film

and points out how films noirs "of the 1940s consistently ignored black Americans," and "the remakes have done so equally"
(Orr 1993, 179). *Bird,* directed by Clint Eastwood and starring
Forest Whitaker, tells the story of jazz great Charlie Parker's
brief and intense life. According to Orr, "it is a retro-movie set
in the noir period, told in flashback with a distinctly *noir* style"
(179). Although the style does hark back to noir, *Bird's* bio-
graphical impulse and lack of criminal activity prevent me from
reading it as a neo-noir.[2] Yet Orr does point to a rich source of
noir story lines, one mined by the 1995 retro-noir film *Devil in
a Blue Dress.*

Directed by Carl Franklin and starring Denzel Washington
as the protagonist, Easy Rawlins, *Devil in a Blue Dress,* based on a
novel by Walter Mosley, revives the hard-boiled detective of
film noir and breathes music, feeling, and soul into him. The
femme fatale in *Devil in a Blue Dress* recalls the 1974 neo-noir
Chinatown. Like the Faye Dunaway character in that film, the
femme fatale is also a femme attrapée. It is not the domestic
realm but an incestuous familial relationship that traps Dunaway's character. In *Devil in a Blue Dress* the femme fatale, the
devil of the film's title, is trapped by her ambiguous racial status. Although of mixed race, she passes as white, and her fi-
ancé's political aspirations are threatened by the truth. In *Chinatown* perverse sexuality poisons the family. In *Devil in a Blue Dress*
perversion rears its head, but race provides the core of the film's
mystery. And, as Janet Maslin indicates in her review, the film
"has the novelty of discovery and the fresh energy to sustain
this material for a long time" (Maslin 1995, B3).

Although her ambiguous racial status provides the mystery
around which the narrative circulates, the femme fatale herself
(Jennifer Beals) seems almost blank. She wears the clothes,
walks the walk, and talks the talk of a femme fatale but does not
manage to arouse much interest or desire. I attribute this to the
film's concern with race, not gender. The femme fatale remains
in the mise en scène but cannot be allowed to steal the scene
as she did in film noir. This retro-noir has other themes to explore. Nevertheless, another female character gets the same
sort of treatment I have identified as typical of film noir. This

character makes love to Easy as her husband sleeps off too many whiskeys in the next room, and provides Easy with information pertaining to the femme fatale. The next day she turns up beaten and murdered, her only apparent crime her insistence on sexual satisfaction from Easy. But the narrative does not insist on that kind of containment for the Beals character. She survives, although the voiceover indicates she will remain forever trapped by her apparent whiteness.

Perhaps noir has exhausted itself on issues relating strictly to gender. Female characters remain central to noir, but they can no longer be neatly contained in categories. Women in recent noirs can be anything from virulent hit-women, such as the one played by Lena Olin in *Romeo is Bleeding* (1995), to femmes fatales who explode my redefinition of the word by surviving and thriving, as Linda Fiorentino's character does in *The Last Seduction* (1995) (which I discuss below). They can be mothers who adopt the garb of a femme fatale in order to eliminate the threat to their family and happiness as the female protagonist does in the neo-noir *Trial By Jury* (1994). Gender remains an issue in neo-noir, just as it remains an issue in our lives. *Devil in a Blue Dress* deals with sex and power, but race provides a new ingredient.

The use of the noir context also marks a change in African-American film, which, as Bernard Weinraub points out, many feel has exhausted the 'hood genre (Weinraub 1995, B1). With *Devil in a Blue Dress* and a number of other recent films such as *Booty Call* (1996), *Waiting to Exhale* (1995), and *White Man's Burden* (1995), black filmmakers move beyond ghetto tales of death and drugs to explore new territory. I have suggested that female characters in recent noirs are even more unpredictable and varied than the characters who populate the Weimar street film and film noir. Carl Franklin makes a similar assertion about African-Americans: "People should realize that black people are not just urban, not just confined to the urban experience, that we are more international, more cosmopolitan and certainly more unpredictable than that" (Weinraub 1995, B1).

Devil in a Blue Dress borrows from film noir, but the differences are telling. Instead of the spare, sharp cinematography of

The Big Heat, *Devil in a Blue Dress* offers a lush, almost soft-focus, but vibrantly energetic vision of an African-American neighborhood in postwar Los Angeles. The dangers that once threatened the white, middle-class home now hover threateningly outside, and occasionally inside, this black neighborhood, mostly in the form of white policemen, white politicians, and their political scams.[3] This retro-noir turns the "white darkness" discussed by Lott inside out and upside down, revealing that much of the evil in the film is racially motivated. The film also shows, with gritty realism, the police interrogation room, with its walls smeared with what looks like blood, and the dark and shadow-filled urban streets. Yet these streets, and much of the film, echo with the strains of a rich assortment of music from the 1940s jazz scene. Rawlins's home and neighborhood appear not as dull, bourgeois traps but as the pot of gold at the end of a rainbow, literally glowing in golden light. *Devil in a Blue Dress* explores territory earlier noirs ignore or cannot imagine, and provides substantial narrative, visual, and aural pleasures along the way. Maslin ends her review by noting, "the film ends peacefully with the slight hint of a sequel on the horizon. A series would be even better." A series of films that explore the black experience of the forties and fifties in the context of Los Angeles, through the eyes of a black private eye played by Denzel Washington, would be welcome to me, as a female spectator and noir aficionada.

German Neo-Noir: *Happy Birthday Turk*

"Sie sprechen aber gut deutsch." (You speak German well.)

—German woman to Turkish-German private detective Kayankaya, who grew up with adoptive German parents and speaks only German, in *Happy Birthday Turk*

A German contribution to the neo-noir canon, *Happy Birthday Turk* (*Happy Birthday Türke*, 1992) also takes race as a dominant concern.[4] Directed by Doris Dörrie and based on the book of the same name written by Jakob Arjouni, *Happy Birthday* features a hard-boiled private detective named Kemal Kayankaya (Hansa Czpionka) attempting to find a missing person in the mean streets of Frankfurt's red-light district. Kayankaya is cut from the same mold as Philip Marlowe and Sam Spade. He displays the hard-drinking, tough-talking, cigarette-smoking allure that Humphrey Bogart made famous in *The Maltese Falcon,* although that lifestyle seems less glamorous in Technicolor than it does in smoky black and white. In the hard-boiled narratives of film noir the private detective stands as the consummate outsider. He does not belong in the homes of his wealthy clients; his code of ethics separates him from those with whom he shares the streets; and the police view him more as a suspect than as a colleague. Kayankaya's position as outsider is further underlined by the fact that, although Turkish, he speaks only German. Unaccepted in mainstream German society because of his ethnicity, his inability to speak Turkish—his linguistic lack—makes him untrustworthy in the eyes of the Turkish community. In this way *Happy Birthday* provides audiences with a classic detective yarn embellished with a concern for race. Whether in retro-noir or neo-noir, the cinema reflects current public discourse on race and ethnicity.

The racism Kayankaya faces every day greets the viewer in the very first sequence of the film, which opens with his landlord drawing a chalk circle around a cigarette butt and a chalk line from the butt along the floor and up the Kayankaya's door, where he circles the apartment number. The landlord appears to view Kayankaya as the source of all the trash in the building. Twice in the course of the film the private detective arrives at his office to find his brass nameplate altered with what appears to be lipstick to read Kamel (German for camel) instead of Kemal Kayankaya. The wife of a retired police officer views him as an exotic and sensual foreigner, belly-dancing for Kayankaya after dinner and asking him if she reminds him of his homeland. A male police receptionist speaks crudely in simple German until Kayankaya identifies himself (falsely) in flawless German as a representative of the Turkish embassy, after which the receptionist becomes fawningly polite. As Carole

Angier notes in her discussion of the film in *Sight and Sound*, "this film about Turks in Germany wasn't made by Turks: the novelist Jakob Arjouni (it's a pen name) is a German; the star, Hansa Czpionka, is a German; Doris Dörrie is of course a German" (Angier 1992, 19). Kayankaya faces these incessant trials and tribulations with bemusement, frustration, and anger; they seem as relentlessly inevitable as police corruption.

If race serves as the dominant subtext, the female characters again provide an enigmatic core to *Happy Birthday*, just as they do in the retro-noir *Devil in a Blue Dress*. A Turkish woman, Ilter (Özay Fecht), hires Kayankaya to find her husband, who has been missing since the day her father-in-law died in a car accident. Ilter is at once mysterious and innocent. She mothers Kayankaya; she cooks him a traditional birthday treat for Turkish children, picks up his messy apartment, and gives him a Turkish-German dictionary as a gift. She also sleeps with him, and insists that "this is the only thing that helps against death." Ilter's husband and father were involved in drug trafficking, and her sister is an addict. But instead of herself succumbing to the vices that surround her, she provides a moral center around which the remainder of the family gathers, and she seeks, unsuccessfully it seems, to draw Kayankaya to that flame as well. In Ilter's final scene in the film, Kayankaya comes to the family apartment to make his last report. Since Ilter first came to his office, he has been trying to return a blue scarf to her. Her response, with a glance at her predominantly silent but powerful mother, is always "not yet." She makes the same remark once more as she joins her family in the sitting room. Ilter seems to want to draw the outsider in, but in typical noir fashion, Kayankaya backs carefully away from that possibility. The final scene in the film shows him dashing off to meet a German prostitute named Margarit.

For critic Angier, another female character in the film, also a prostitute, is most fully realized. According to Angier, "The character who really moved me was Hanna (Meret Beker): the hopeless, corrupted, childish German prostitute. This was a superb portrait: completely rounded, completely understood" (Angier 1992, 19). Angier asserts that Dörrie's camera "dwells on Hanna . . . suggesting a hidden emotional truth about her film" (19). It is difficult, as a woman watching films directed by women, not to look for those hidden emotional truths that seem to address a shared point of view.[5] In a sense, I agree with Angier. The character of Hanna does seem fully realized and unenigmatic. Her future beyond the narrative of the film is easy to predict—dissipation, continued drug addiction, prostitution, and an early death. The future in store for Ilter and her family seems less certain, but also has more potential. Ilter and her mother, as they gather the family into the living room, embody the only strength and morality the world seems to offer. It is a morality the hard-boiled detective seeks to preserve and protect, even as he eludes its grasp.

Director Dörrie often comes under fire both in the United States and Europe for not dealing specifically with issues of gender. While I too would like to see more women directors explore issues of female identity, it seems to me unfair to expect them to assume the burden of readjusting the male-centered film industry. The only film noir directed by a woman, Ida Lupino's *The Hitch-Hiker* (1953), featured an all-male cast, with the exception of a waitress with a bit part. *Happy Birthday Turk* might not address the female spectator, but it does provide an entertaining, informative, and moving portrait of the racism Turkish nationals experience in Germany, of the seedy underbelly of the city of Frankfurt, of police corruption and racism, of familial loyalty and love, and of a hard-boiled detective who, like Raymond Chandler's ideal detective, goes down the mean streets but is not himself mean.

U.S. Neo-Noir: Survival of the Fittest in *The Last Seduction*

"They're soft, I thought they'd be stiff."

—Bridget, remarking on the feel of a bundle of drug money, in *The Last Seduction*

In *The Last Seduction* (1993), directed by John Dahl, the femme fatale emphatically rejects the noir tradition of the containment of female agency.[6] Linda Fiorentino plays Bridget Gregory, a vibrantly bitchy and hard-boiled femme fatale capable of using every trick and trope in the noir playbook to manipulate and murder men and amass her fortune. Yet she rides off into a rainy New York afternoon in a chauffeur-driven limousine at the end of the film, leaving one man behind bars for the murder of another—a crime she committed. *The Last Seduction* refers to film noir in every twist and turn of the complicated plot; in the shadow-filled shades of blue that replace the grays of black-and-white cinematography; in the atmospheric thunder, lightning, and rain that punctuate the action at crucial intervals; and in the ease with which the femme fatale manipulates men, including her husband, her lover, her new boss, the police, and a few private detectives. Bridget gazes at men through a concealing veil of dark hair, surrounds herself in a haze of cigarette smoke, and drinks manhattans at the bar and straight Bushmill's whiskey at home. She exemplifies and magnifies the characteristics that once guaranteed a violent end for the noir femme fatale.

The Last Seduction first presents Bridget verbally abusing a group of phone salesmen (they do seem to be primarily men) in a smoky, blue-hued office. No establishing shot delineates the overall space of the room, so the spectator never really understands the organization of the office. Off-angle, tight shots of Bridget striding between desks, of her leaning over to harass an inefficient or overly sympathetic salesman of commemorative coins seem to locate the spectator in a chair behind a desk at the phone banks. Intercut with these shots, implying simultaneity, another sequence shows her husband, Clay (Bill Pullman), bumbling his way through a drug sale in some seedy New York setting. From the inception of the narrative, her power and proficiency stand opposed to his lack of confidence and capability. Bridget, a wife and potentially a femme attrapée, like Laurie in *Gun Crazy* cannot be contained. Her primacy in a battle of wits with her husband or anyone else seems overdetermined. Bridget's proficiency with language constitutes both her vocation and her avocation and contributes to that primacy.

As Stephen Lamb points out, one of the first femmes fatales given a voice, Lola (Marlene Dietrich) in the Weimar *Blue Angel,* displays her command of language. According to Lamb, "Lola's manipulation of language . . . signifies her usurping of his [Rath's] territory, her acquisition of control over him" (Lamb 1995, 125). Similarly, as discussed in chapter 8, in *The Maltese Falcon* Brigid O'Shaughnessy earns Sam Spade's grudging admiration for her ability to make language work for her. Like Brigid O'Shaughnessy, Bridget Gregory in *The Last Seduction* proves to be an adept liar and a person with impressive verbal acuity. Whereas Brigid O'Shaughnessy's assumed names were designed to emphasize her supposed innocence (Miss LeBlanc) or her beauty (Miss Wonderly), Bridget Gregory calls herself Wendy Kroy. Dropping the *-dy* from *Wendy* leaves an anagram for her beloved New York. She works as a supervisor in various phone-sales businesses, an occupation that relies on spoken language to convey the allure of the product being promoted. In the course of the film Bridget writes a note that can only be read by holding it up to a mirror, and signs her name to a document facing away from her. The femme fatale, once she begins to speak, progresses from wisecracks to complicated lies to tricks with written language, from an aptitude for spoken words to complete command of the sign system. In one instance, Bridget even uses the signs and symbols of a schoolgirl crush doodled onto a note pad and personalized with her lover's name to convince him of the sincerity of her affections.

As I have shown, many critics run into difficulties when trying to account for the femme fatale's motivation. I find she usually says what she wants and why. As I show in chapter 9, both Hirsch and a *Newsweek* reviewer express confusion about what motivates Laurie in *Gun Crazy,* when she makes it perfectly clear she does not want to live the small-town life and tells Bart, "I want things, lots of things." Similarly, in a review of *The Last Seduction,* Kim Newman suggests Bridget's "motives are never fully explained, the implication is that Bridget really is the thoroughgoing bitch she claims to be" (Newman 1994, 44). But Bridget's motivation parallels Laurie's. She also wants things, lots of things. She is unwilling to settle for getting by in New York; she wants to enjoy the good life and stops at nothing to obtain it. Unlike Laurie, who does seem to care for Bart despite her manipulation of him, Bridget seems to have little use for the men she involves in her duplicitous schemes. Newman notes that Fiorentino (as Bridget) "always stirs in enough underlying contempt to signal the character's belief that the fools she dupes are not worth the effort of a really convincing imposture" (44). None of the men in *The Last Seduction* seem equal to Bridget, and her sexual prowess matches her verbal acuity. Although she expertly manipulates words when necessary, Bridget does not mince them. When her lover presses her about the nature of their relationship, she tells him he is her "designated fuck" and if he does not perform his duties correctly she will "designate someone else." Bridget's control of language, of her sexuality, and eventually of her destiny make her the epitome of a neo-noir femme fatale.

John Orr notes that with *Body Heat* (1981), American cinema begins to atone for "an earlier generation of noir movies in which female crime and desire are necessarily punished" (Orr 1993, 175). Orr goes on to assert that "the punishment of the woman has lost its mythical *cachet*" (175). Such punishment may have lost its cachet, yet the ending of *Body Heat*, like that of *The Last Seduction*, in which the femme fatale enjoys the fruits of her avaricious and murderous acts, still surprises the viewer. The shock of surprise, the survival of a type of woman the cinemagoer has seen destroyed in countless narratives, might be especially pleasurable for a female spectator and might even be designed with her in mind. I noted how Laurie Starr's inevitable demise at the end of *Gun Crazy* evokes a certain emotional ambivalence in the spectator. The inevitable containment of female desire in the final reel of a film noir gives way in neo-noir to the possibility of a female character "who cannot be appropriated, who cannot be conquered . . . or bought off, or punished" (175). Bridget asserts her financial, sexual, and personal desires and does not merely get away with it, but thrives. The femme fatale proves more fatal to others than to herself. No wonder *The Last Seduction* seems like a breath of fresh air after hours of seeing women like Bridget engineer not only their own financial and sexual satisfaction but their demise. Punished by containment in the Weimar street film, and by destruction and death in film noir, the wholly assertive, sexually uninhibited female character comes into her own in *The Last Seduction.* In *Jackie Brown* (1997), she continues on her way. I, for one, cannot wait to see where she is headed.

NOTES

Introduction

1. For a concise critique of Agger's conception of feminist cultural studies, see Smith 1996.

Chapter 1

1. Of course, Mulvey adds that by identifying with active male characters, female spectators can gain access to their repressed masculinity (Mulvey 1989, 37).

Chapter 2

1. Sirk's pastel-colored, brightly lit melodramas reject the ambiguity that infuses the visual style of film noir, replacing it with a filmic reality that drips with irony.

2. In *The Fatal Woman*, Maxfield seems to concur with my redefinition of femme fatale and includes *Thelma and Louise* (1991) in his final chapter. Thelma and Louise are fatal to one man, the one who rapes Louise; but, more importantly, they engineer their own deaths.

Chapter 3

1. As McCormick also notes, that promise has still not been added to the U.S. Constitution.

2. Similar statistics fuel the male identity crisis of the film noir years (1942–1958) in the United States.

3. Gleber (1997) brilliantly rereads the *Symphony of the City*, locating the female flânerie on the streets of the metropolis.

Chapter 4

1. "Der Zauber der Straße wird hier mit dem Zauber des Kinos selbst identifiziert: gleich in der ersten Szene beobachtet der Mann an der Wand Licht- und Schattenspiele von pulsierendem Leben wie eine Filmprojektion" (Kaes 1993, 60). Translations from the German are my own unless otherwise noted.

2. Although the verbal description of this heart-shaped mask makes it sound obtrusive, it is visually subtle.

3. Brennicke and Hembus provide a still of this image, and suggest it was "plagiarized" from *Von Morgens bis Mitternacht* (Brennicke and Hembus 1983, 221, 229). The image is extremely difficult to see in video versions.

4. Max Schreck, who still strikes fear into my heart as *Nosferatu* (1922), now arouses pity as the old, blind man. In German, Schreck means fright or terror.

5. The version of the film I work with here is available from Video Yesteryear. The titles are in English.

6. The English-language version I acquired supposedly told "the story of a night in Paris." I can only speculate that a night spent *in Paris* added to the potential titillation the audience might hope to enjoy.

7. As I mentioned earlier, the imaginary spectator is "the construction of patriarchal ideology, the one to whom the film is addressed" (Creed 1989, 20–21).

Chapter 5

1. "Ich flehe den Himmel an, daß mein Antrag erhört wird, daß du wieder zu deinem Kind zurückkommst, das von nichts weiß und jeden Tag nach seinem Vater ausschaut, von dem es weiß, daß er sehr weit weg in einem fremden Land ist . . . " The Friedrich Wilhelm Murnau Stiftung in Wiesbaden assisted me by providing a German title list for *Variety*. All further references in the text to this source will be parenthetical (FWMS).

2. "Ich habe Sehnsucht nach dir. . . . Vergiß nicht, daß du ohne mich noch heute mit den Schaustellern herumziehen würdest."

3. "Wie ein Vampir hat diese Frau von ihm Besitz ergriffen, und alle Wellen der Lust und Leidenschaft schossen über ihnen zusammen." Quoted from an information sheet from FWMS. According to Ephraim Katz, Dupont emigrated to the United States in 1933 and continued to write screenplays and direct Hollywood productions, including the 1951 psychological film noir *The Scarf* (Katz 1994, 366).

4. See my discussion of the versions of this film later in this chapter.

5. Huller engages in these tasks more happily than the other "wives" discussed thus far, perhaps because he enjoys his spouse's animated attention.

6. The desirability of these male characters might also appeal to a homosexual male spectator, but that intriguing possibility belongs in another study.

7. This information is according to Ephraim Katz in *The Film Encyclopedia*. Katz also notes that Freund ended his career as the chief cinematographer for Desilu productions, perhaps overseeing the shooting of *I Love Lucy* (Katz 1994, 454).

8. "Sprachlose Attraktionen, die nur auf die Schaulust der Zuschauer spekulieren, gab es . . . in *Variety*, wenn etwa die Kamera hoch über den

Köpfen der Zuschauer mit dem Trapez selbst auf- und abschwingt, so daß Lichter zu verfließenden Punkten und Strichen werden und der Film abstrakte Qualität annimmt: ein sich selbst genügsames sinnliches Spiel der optischen Sphäre mit Licht und Bewegung."

9. Since Huller is the man responsible for catching Artinelli every evening in a dangerous trapeze act, we have to wonder about Artinelli's choice of Berta Maria as a lover.

10. I had the good fortune to see this version while visiting the Friedrich Wilhelm Murnau Stiftung in Wiesbaden.

Chapter 6

1. The actual release date of *Asphalt* remains unclear, and is often reported as 1928/29. Most of the German film reviews date from early in 1929.

2. According to Katz, the Jewish Pommer left Germany in 1933. He returned to Germany in 1946 to restore "the shattered German film industry" (Katz 1994, 1091). He moved back to Hollywood in 1956 and remained there until his death in 1966. During his exile in Hollywood, Pommer produced *Dance Girl Dance* (1939), directed by Dorothy Arzner.

3. Kettlehut was also involved in that superb cinematic document of New Objectivity, *The Symphony of a Great City.*

4. Gudrun Weiss at the Friedrich Wilhelm Murnau Stiftung (FWMS) in Wiesbaden provided this document for me.

5. "Milieu der Straße, aber im Dienst der symbolischen Überhöhung; Realismus war durchdachtes Konstrukt, eine besonders schwere Aufgabe im Studio."

6. "Die Straße wird dann ein Symbol des menschlichen Lebens—ein unendliches Ineinanderfluten von Schicksalen."

7. "[E]s läßt sich nichts 'moderneres' denken als die verblüffende Lebendigkeit der Straßenszenen: die Kamera beherrscht alles, wählt aus, isoliert, sie arbeitet wie das menschliche Auge, ist von einer immensen Wachheit. . . . 1927 hat der Stummfilm seinen großen klassischen Stil gefunden. Keine leeren Stellen mehr, kein Theater mehr: das Kino war zu allem fähig."

8. Quoted in Ilona Brennicke and Joe Hembus, eds., *Klassiker des Deutschen Stummfilms 1910–1933* (Munich: Goldmann Verlag, 1983), 176.

9. Germany's film industry at the end of the 1920s resembles Hollywood more than most would think; it utilized both the studio system and classical style of editing commonly associated with Hollywood.

10. "Schade, daß, wie so oft in Deutschland, das technische Verständnis sich auf Kosten des Wissens um die geistigen Bedeutungen auslebt. Asphalt auch hier." Gudrun Weiss at the FWMS provided me with the *Verleihkatalog des deutschen Institut für Filmkunde.*

11. As often occurs with silent films, there are multiple versions of *Asphalt*. In one version, the mother is amazed at all that happens in a day; in another, she comments about how the newspaper contains only sensational stories.

12. Some silent-film aficionados will recall the importance of the caged bird in the great 1923 silent film *Greed*, directed by Eric von Stroheim, and adapted from Frank Norris's novel *McTeague*.

13. The diegetic male spectator exists within the world of the film's story. The extradiegetic spectator sits in the movie audience and watches the story unfold.

14. "Da wird die Staatsgewalt erfreulich korumpiert durch Eleganz, durch Pelze, durch gleißende Stoffe, durch samtene Atmosphäre in einem Boudoir und Blicke unter Künstlichen Wimpern. Man spürt: es sind die Augen, die verführt werden."

15. "Du gefällst mir."

16. "Ein wahres Lehrstück des Kinos."

17. In the neo-noir *Romeo is Bleeding*, Lena Olin plays femme fatale Mona. Mona displays a blatant seductivity and physical prowess that make her seem like the 1993 version of Else. Else's eventual self-sacrifice remains unthinkable for Mona, whose murderous drives are finally contained by numerous policemen simultaneously, and fearfully, emptying their guns into her.

18. Kracauer's dominant image, that of the man with his head in his mother's lap or bosom, does occur in *Asphalt*, as Holk cries in his mother's lap before his father takes him off to jail.

19. See my discussion in chapter 8 of *The Maltese Falcon* (1941), which ends similarly, with Sam Spade promising to wait for femme fatale Brigid O'Shaughnessy before the bars of the elevator, and then prison, separate them. But by 1941 the biting sarcasm in Bogie's voice reveals noir cynicism at the concept of such a "quasi" happy ending.

20. I see no evidence that Else is a prostitute.

21. Kracauer's description of film noir holds frighteningly true for the neo-noir as well, but perhaps most pointedly for the genre of violent, urban black films typified by *Boyz N the Hood* (1991) and *Clockers* (1995).

22. For a discussion of both versions of *M*, see Edward Dimendberg, "From Berlin to Bunker Hill: Urban Space, Late Modernity, and Film Noir in Fritz Lang's and Joseph Losey's *M*," *Wide Angle* 19.4 (1997): 62–93.

Chapter 7

1. Silver and Ward credit Nino Frank with coining the term *film noir* in his essay "Un nouveau genre 'policier': L'adventure criminelle," *L'Ecran Français 61*, no. 28.8 (1946): 8–9, 14.

2. According to Silver and Ward, Borde and Chaumeton added a postscript to a later edition of their book identifying *Kiss Me Deadly* as the "fas-

cinating and dusky conclusion" to film noir (Silver and Ward 1992, 372).

3. Others, including Thomas Schatz and Robert Ottoson, have also noted the importance of *Citizen Kane* to film noir.

4. Silver and Ward provide a succinct discussion of these ongoing debates (Silver and Ward 1992, 372–85 [app. C]). I devote only a few pages to them.

5. Porfirio's essay makes a sound argument for film noir as a form of cinematic existentialism, with the individual protagonist who must recognize the "meaninglessness of existence" and "discover the ability to create one's own values" (Porfiro 1976, 216).

Chapter 8

1. Nolan finds it unfortunate that the proposed sequel was never filmed. I do not share his unbridled optimism that the further adventures would have provided the visual and narrative pleasures of the original, but admit the concept sounds intriguing.

2. Richard Dyer speculates on Rita Hayworth's potential disruption of male narrative control in *Gilda* (Dyer 1980).

3. For a frame-by-frame breakdown of the film, including dialogue, see Anobile 1974. The sequence in which Cairo and Brigid spar is found on pp. 90–92.

Chapter 9

1. Recently released on video, *Gun Crazy* is part of the gangster collection from the CBS/FOX company.

2. The film also features some remarkable deep-focus photography, and a superb long take that rivals those of Hitchcock and Welles.

3. Bordwell and Thompson define plot in narrative film as "all the events that are directly presented to us," and contrast that with story (also called the diegesis), which is "all the events we see and hear, plus all those we infer or assume to have occurred" (Bordwell and Thompson 1993, 496, 497).

4. In an eyeline match, "shot A presents someone looking offscreen; shot B shows us what is being looked at. In neither shot are *both* looker and object present" (Bordwell and Thompson 1993, 265).

5. Kitses details the censors' reactions to this sequence, and notes that director Lewis maintains no pun was intended (Kitses 1996, 41).

6. By the end of the film, Ruby has had a third child. Her husband is again not present, this time out of town on business.

7. For a still showing Laurie and Miss Sifert facing off, see *Bright Lights Film Journal* no. 12 (Spring 1994): 6.

8. Kitses reads Bart's shooting of Laurie as a reaffirmation of Bart's passionate bond with her, suggesting Bart resolves his ambivalent affair "with a final, reluctant embrace of 'action'" (Kitses 1996, 66).

Chapter 10

1. See my own discussion of *The Big Heat*, which hinges more on the domestic realm and the character development of the male protagonist (Wager 1995).

2. Marlon Brando is Jocelyn Brando's brother.

3. Lang elaborates with an example from "the horrible sexual crime" in *M*: "(*e*)*veryone* in the audience—even the one who doesn't *dare* allow himself to understand what really happened to that poor child—has a horrible feeling that runs over his back. But everybody has a *different* feeling, because everybody *imagines* the most horrible thing that could happen to her" (quoted in Bogdanovich 1967, 86). I often wish other directors would follow Lang's lead with regard to on-screen violence.

4. McArthur's (1992) analysis of *The Big Heat* includes a discussion of the novel upon which the film is based and a particularly astute analysis of the use of dissolves in the film.

5. In the junkyard sequence Selma reaches out to Bannion "in the depth of his despair," and according to McArthur, begins his reintegration into society (McArthur 1992, 67).

6. Beware of shoddy secondary sources. In the impressively titled *Film Noir: A Comprehensive, Illustrated Reference to Movies, Terms and Persons* (Jefferson, N.C.: McFarland, 1995), Michael Stephens identifies Debbie as Lagana's girlfriend, and says she is having an affair with Stone. Debbie is clearly identified, by Lagana and others, as Stone's girlfriend, although she does express interest in Bannion. Stephens claims Debbie's "relationships with both Lagana and Stone is [*sic*] masochistic," and that she "positively revels in her debasement," a comment that makes me wonder which film he watched (p. 42).

7. When watching this sequence, note how the coffeepot is innocuously present in almost every shot leading up to its use. Lang comments, "[t]he whole thing wouldn't have been possible unless the coffee was a hundred degrees. So while the gang is playing poker in one room . . . I showed that the coffee on the stove is steaming" (quoted in Bogdanovich 1967, 87). Lang worried about the criticism of wives who "have thrown hot coffee in their husband's faces and were disappointed with the result" (87).

8. Lang insists Debbie "could have had plastic surgery," but I doubt Debbie would have considered the partial restoration of her looks enough (quoted in Bogdanovich 1967, 87).

9. The big heat, slang for intense police activity, will follow the release of Duncan's letter, which details the activities of Lagana's crime syndicate.

10. According to McArthur, the final sequence of an earlier version of the screenplay has Bannion "entering a car which will take him to have breakfast with his daughter" (McArthur 1992, 77).

11. "Sie stehen zwischen den Systemen, versuchen zu vermitteln oder

aus dem Konflikt das Beste für sich zu machen, schlagen sich auf die eine oder die andere Seite, werden zerrieben."

Chapter 12

1. I think, with the recent explosion of neo- and retro-noirs, that bracketing off the seventies noirs from this new wave of nineties noirs might help clarify the terminology further.

2. Perhaps I should say relative lack of criminal activity, as Parker's heroin addiction might be read as criminal. Orr suggests heroin takes the place of the femme fatale, killing off Bird and his music.

3. In one instance a white L.A. cop assures Rawlins that it can be made to look as though Rawlins committed a crime, whether he did or not, and that this has been done many times before. The Fuhrman tapes at the O. J. Simpson trial provide a stinging, real-life commentary on the assertion.

4. *The Glass Heaven (Der gläserne Himmel)*, a 1987 film by Nina Gosse, also exhibits noir influences.

5. I find myself looking for the same sort of connections in the films of Kathyrn Bigelow, who like Dörrie succeeds in making big-budget, often violent, and usually successful mainstream films.

6. Dahl also directed the neo-noir *Red Rock West* (1993), set in rural Wyoming, which features a wife who is also a femme fatale.

REFERENCES

Agger, Ben. 1992. *Cultural Studies as Critical Theory.* London: Falmer Press.

Angier, Carole. 1992. "Always the Outsider." *Sight and Sound* 1.9: 16–19.

Anobile, Richard J., ed. 1974. *The Maltese Falcon.* New York: Universe Books.

Astor, Mary. 1971. *A Life on Film.* New York: Delacorte Press.

Barlow, John D. 1982. *German Expressionist Film.* Twayne's Filmmakers Series. Boston: Twayne.

Belton, John. 1994. *American Cinema/American Culture.* New York: McGraw-Hill.

Bogdanovich, Peter. 1967. *Fritz Lang in America.* New York: Praeger.

Borde, Raymond, and Etienne Chaumeton. 1955. *Panorama du film noir américain, 1941–1953.* Paris: Flammarion.

Bordwell, David, Janet Staiger, and Kristin Thompson. 1985. *The Classical Hollywood Cinema: Film Style and Mode of Production to 1960.* New York: Columbia University Press.

Bordwell, David, and Kristin Thompson. 1993. *Film Art: An Introduction.* 4th ed. New York: McGraw-Hill.

Brennicke, Ilona, and Joe Hembus, eds. 1983. *Klassiker des deutschen Stummfilms, 1910–1933.* Munich: Goldmann Verlag.

Bridenthal, Renate, Atina Grossmann, and Marion Kaplan, eds. 1984. *When Biology Became Destiny: Women in Weimar and Nazi Germany.* New York: Monthly Review Press.

Brooks, Peter. 1976. *The Melodramatic Imagination: Balzac, Henry James, Melodrama, and the Mode of Excess.* New Haven: Yale University Press.

Chafe, William H. 1991. *The Paradox of Change: American Women in the Twentieth Century.* New York: Oxford University Press.

Christopher, Nicholas. 1997. *Somewhere in the Night: Film Noir and the American City.* New York: Free Press.

Cohen, Mitchell S. 1974. "The Actor: Villains and Victims." *Film Comment* 10:6 (November-December): 27–29.

Conners, Martin, and Julia Furtaw, eds. 1995. VideoHound's *Golden Movie Retriever.* Detroit: Visible Ink Press.

Cook, David A. 1981. *A History of Narrative Film.* New York: Norton.

Cowie, Elizabeth. 1993. "*Film Noir* and Women." In *Shades of Noir: A Reader,* ed. Joan Copjec, 121–65. London: Verso.

Creed, Barbara. 1989. "Individual Responses." *Camera Obscura* 20–21 (1989): 132–37.

Dahlke, Günther, and Günter Karl, eds. 1993. *Deutsche Spielfilme von den Anfängen bis 1933: Ein Filmführer.* Berlin: Henschel Verlag.

"Deadly Is the Female." 1950. *Newsweek* 23.2 (9 January): 70.

Dimendberg, Edward. 1997. "From Berlin to Bunker Hill: Urban Space, Late Modernity, and Film Noir in Fritz Lang's and Joseph Losey's M." *Wide Angle* 19.4: 62–93.

Doane, Mary Ann. 1989. "Individual Responses." *Camera Obscura* 20–21: 142–46.

———. 1991. *Femmes Fatales: Feminism, Film Theory, Psychoanalysis.* New York: Routledge.

Dyer, Richard. 1980. "Resistance through Charisma: Rita Hayworth and *Gilda.*" In *Women in Film Noir,* ed. E. Ann Kaplan, 91–99. London: British Film Institute.

———. 1993. "Homosexuality in Film Noir." In *The Matter of Images: Essays on Representations,* 52–72. London: Routledge.

Eisner, Lotte H. 1969. *The Haunted Screen: Expressionism in the German Cinema and the Influence of Max Reinhardt.* Trans. from the French by Roger Greaves. Berkeley: University of California Press.

Elsaesser, Thomas. 1986. "Lulu and the Meter Man: Pabst's *Pandora's Box* (1929)." In *German Film and Literature: Adaptations and Transformations,* ed. Eric Rentschler, 40–59. New York: Methuen.

Fischetti, Renate. 1992. *Das neue Kino: Acht Porträts von deutschen Regisseurinnen.* Frankfurt am Main: Tende.

Gaines, Jane. 1990. "Women and Representation: Can We Enjoy Alternative Pleasure?" In *Issues in Feminist Film Criticism,* ed. Patricia Erens, 75–92. Bloomington: Indiana University Press.

Garncarz, Joseph. 1993. "Hollywood in Germany: Die Rolle des amerikanischen Films in Deutschland: 1925–1990." In *Der deutsche Film: Aspekte seiner Geschichte von den Anfängen bis zur Gegenwart,* ed. Uli Jung, 167–213. Trier: Wissenschaftlicher Verlag.

Gehler, Fred. 1993. "*Varieté.*" In *Deutsche Spielfilme von den Anfängen bis 1933,* ed. Günther Dahlke and Günter Karl, 120–22. Berlin: Henschel Verlag.

Gleber, Anke. 1997. "Female Flanerie and the *Symphony of the City.*" In *Women in the Metropolis: Gender and Modernity in Weimar Culture,* ed. Katharina von Ankum, 67–88. Berkeley: University of California Press.

Grafe, Frieda, and Enno Patalas. 1969. "Nicht nur Pick & Pabst," in *Filmkritik.* Quoted in *Klassiker des deutschen Stummfilms 1910–1933,* ed. Ilona Brennicke and Joe Hembus. Munich: Goldmann Verlag, 1983.

Hales, Barbara. 1996. "Woman as Sexual Criminal: Weimar Constructions of the Criminal *Femme Fatale.*" *Women in German Yearbook* 12: 101–21.

Hall, Jasmine Yong. 1990. "Jameson, Genre, and Gumshoes: The Maltese

Falcon as Inverted Romance." In *The Cunning Craft: Original Essays on Detective Fiction and Contemporary Literary Theory,* ed. Ronald G. Walker and June M. Frazer, 109–19. Macomb: Western Illinois University Press.

Hall, Mordaunt. 1926. "A German Masterpiece." *New York Times,* 28 June, 15:5.

———. 1927. "An Expressionistic Study." *New York Times,* 6 September, 34:3.

———. 1928. "The Best Pictures of the Past Year." *New York Times,* 1 January, 7:1.

———. 1930. "The Susceptible Policeman." *New York Times,* 6 May, 33:4.

Hanisch, Michael. 1993. *"Asphalt."* In *Deutsche Spielfilme von den Anfängen bis 1933,* ed. Günther Dahlke and Günter Karl, 181–82. Berlin: Henschel Verlag.

Harvey, Silvia. 1978. "Woman's Place: The Absent Family in Film Noir." In *Women in Film Noir,* ed. E. Ann Kaplan, 22–34. London: British Film Institute.

Hirsch, Foster. 1981. *The Dark Side of the Screen: Film Noir.* San Diego: A. S. Barnes.

Huston, John. 1980. *An Open Book.* New York: Knopf.

Jacobsen, Wolfgang, Anton Kaes, and Hans Helmut Prinzler, eds. 1993. *Geschichte des deutschen Films.* Stuttgart: J. B. Metzler.

Johann, Ernst, and Jörg Junker. 1970. *German Cultural History of the Last Hundred Years.* Munich: Nymphenburger Verlagshandlung.

Kaes, Anton, 1989. *From Hitler to Heimat: The Return of History as Film.* Cambridge, Mass.: Harvard University Press.

———. 1993. "Film in der Weimarer Republik." In *Geschichte des deutschen Films,* ed. Wolfgang Jacobsen, Anton Kaes, and Hans Helmut Prinzler, 39–100. Stuttgart: J. B. Metzler.

Kaplan, E. Ann, ed. 1978. *Women in Film Noir.* London: British Film Institute.

Katz, Ephraim. 1994. *The Film Encyclopedia.* New York: Harper Perennial.

Kauffmann, Stanley. 1991. "Not So Crazy." *New Republic,* 24 June: 26–27.

Kitses, Jim. 1996. *Gun Crazy.* BFI Film Classics. London: British Film Institute.

Koonz, Claudia. 1987. *Mothers in the Fatherland: Women, the Family, and Nazi Politics.* New York: St. Martin's.

Kracauer, Siegfried. 1929. *Frankfurter Zeitung,* Abendausgabe, 28 March. Quoted from the *Verleihkatalog des deutschen Institut für Filmkunde,* 42.

———. 1946. "Hollywood's Terror Films: Do They Reflect an American State of Mind?" *Commentary* 2.2 (August).

———. 1947. *From Caligari to Hitler: A Psychological History of the German Film.* Princeton: Princeton University Press.

Krutnik, Frank. 1991. *In a Lonely Street: Film Noir, Genre, Masculinity.* London: Routledge.

Lamb, Stephen. 1995. "Woman's Nature?: Images of Women in *The Blue*

Angel, Pandora's Box, Kuhle Wampe and *Girls in Uniform*." In *Visions of the "Neue Frau": Women and the Visual Arts in Weimar Germany*, ed. Marsha Meskimmon and Shearer West, 124–42. Aldershot, England: Scolar Press.

Laplanche, Jean, and Jean-Bertrand Pontalis. 1986. "Fantasy and the Origins of Sexuality: Retrospect, 1986." In *Formations of Fantasy*, ed. Victor Burgin, James Donald, and Cora Kaplan, 5–34. New York: Methuen.

Lapsley, Robert, and Michael Westlake. 1988. *Film Theory: An Introduction*. Manchester: Manchester University Press.

Leff, Leonard J., and Jerold L. Simmons. 1990. *The Dame in the Kimono: Hollywood, Censorship, and the Production Code from the 1920s to the 1960s*. New York: Grove Weidenfeld.

Manvell, Roger, and Heinrich Fraenkel. 1971. *The German Cinema*. London: J. M. Dent and Sons.

Mänz, Peter. N.d. "Metropolis, Berlin, New York-Neubabelsberg: Der Architekt Erich Kettelhut." *Asphalt, UFA Magazin*, no. 7. N.p.

Maslin, Janet. 1995. "A Black Gumshoe Who's Also Noir." *New York Times*, 29 Sept. 1995: B3.

Maxfield, James. 1996. *The Fatal Woman: Sources of Male Anxiety in American Film Noir, 1941–1991*. Madison, N.J.: Fairleigh Dickinson Univerity Press.

Mayne, Judith. 1993. *Cinema and Spectatorship*. London: Routledge.

McArthur, Colin. 1992. *The Big Heat*. BFI Film Classics. London: British Film Institute.

McCormick, Richard W. 1993. "From Caligari to Dietrich: Sexual, Social and Cinematic Discourses in Weimar Film." *Signs* (Spring): 640–68.

McHale, Brian. 1987. *Postmodernist Fiction*. London: Routledge.

Meskimmon, Marsha, and Shearer West, eds. 1995. *Visions of the "Neue Frau": Women and the Visual Arts in Weimar Germany*. Aldershot, England: Scolar Press.

Monaco, James. 1981. *How to Read a Film: The Art, Technology, Language, History, and Theory of Film and Media*. New York: Oxford University Press.

Mulvey, Laura. 1989. "Notes on Sirk and Melodrama." In *Visual and Other Pleasures*, 39–48. Bloomington: Indiana University Press.

———. 1989. "Visual Pleasure and Narrative Cinema." In *Visual and Other Pleasures*, 14–26. Bloomington: Indiana University Press.

———. 1989. "Afterthoughts Inspired by Duel in the Sun." In *Visual and Other Pleasures*, 29–38. Bloomington: Indiana University Press.

———. 1992. *Citizen Kane*. BFI Film Classics. London: British Film Institute.

Munson, Anthony K. 1982. "Dirnentragödie." In *Film and Politics in the Weimar Republic*, ed. Thomas Plummer et al., 62–64. New York: Holmes and Meier.

Murray, Bruce. 1990. *Film and the German Left in the Weimar Republic: From Caligari to Kuhle Wampe*. Austin: University of Texas Press.

Naremore, James. 1995. "American Film Noir: The History of an Idea." *Film Quarterly* 49.2 (Winter): 12.

Newman, Kim. 1994. "The Last Seduction." *Sight and Sound* 4.8: 44.

Nolan, William F. 1965. *John Huston, King Rebel*. Los Angeles: Sherbourne Press.

Orr, John. 1993. *Cinema and Modernity*. Cambridge: Polity Press.

Ott, Frederick W. 1986. *The Great German Films*. Secaucus, N.J.: Citadel Press.

Palmer, R. Barton. 1994. *Hollywood's Dark Cinema: The American Film Noir*. Twayne's Filmmakers Series. New York: Twayne.

Patalas, Enno, Frieda Grafe, Hans Helmut Prinzler, and Peter Syr. 1976. *Fritz Lang*. Reihe Film 7. Munich: Carl Hanser.

Petro, Patrice. 1989. *Joyless Streets: Women and Melodramatic Representation in Weimar Germany*. Princeton: Princeton University Press.

Place, Janey. 1980. "Women in Film Noir." In *Women in Film Noir*, ed. E. Ann Kaplan, 35–67. London: British Film Institute.

Place, J. A., and L. S. Peterson. 1976. "Some Visual Motifs of *Film Noir*." In *Movies and Methods: An Anthology*, ed. Bill Nichols, 325–38. Berkeley: University of California Press.

Plummer, Thomas, Bruce Murray, Linda Schulte-Sasse, Anthony K. Munson, and Laurie Loomis Perry, eds. 1982. *Film and Politics in the Weimar Republic*. New York: Holmes and Meier.

Polan, Dana. 1986. *Power and Paranoia: History, Narrative, and the American Cinema, 1940–1950*. New York: Columbia University Press.

Porfirio, Robert G. 1976. "No Way Out: Existential Motifs in the Film Noir." *Sight and Sound* 45.4: 212–17.

Rentschler, Eric, ed. 1986. *German Film and Literature: Adaptations and Transformations*. New York: Methuen.

———, ed. 1988. *West German Filmmakers on Film: Visions and Voices*. New York: Holmes and Meier.

Richardson, Carl. 1992. *Autopsy: An Element of Realism in Film Noir*. Metuchen, N.J.: Scarecrow Press.

Schatz, Thomas. 1981. *Hollywood Genres: Formulas, Filmmaking, and the Studio System*. Philadelphia: Temple University Press.

Schlüpmann, Heide. 1990. *Unheimlichkeit des Blicks: Das Drama des frühen deutschen Kinos*. Frankfurt am Main: Stroemfeld /Roter Stern.

Schrader, Paul. 1972. "Notes on Film Noir." *Film Comment* 8.1: 8–13.

Silver, Alain, and Elizabeth Ward, eds. 1992. *Film Noir: An Encyclopedic Reference to the American Style*. Woodstock, N.Y.: Overlook Press.

Silverman, Kaja. 1992. *Male Subjectivity at the Margins*. New York: Routledge.

Smith, Sabine H. 1996. "Sexual Violence in German Culture: Rereading and Rewriting the Tradition." Ph.D. dissertation, University of California.

Stacey, Jackie. 1994. *Star Gazing: Hollywood Cinema and Female Spectatorship.* London: Routledge.

Thomas, Deborah. 1992. "How Hollywood Deals with the Deviant Male." In *The Movie Book of Film Noir,* ed. Ian Cameron, 59–70. London: Studio Vista.

Thönnessen, Werner. 1973. *The Emancipation of Women: The Rise and Decline of the Women's Movement in German Social Democracy, 1863–1933.* Trans. Joris de Bres. London: Pluto Press.

Wager, Jans. 1995. "The Big Heat." *Bright Lights Film Journal,* no. 14 (March): 23–26.

Weinraub, Bernard. 1995. "Black Film Makers Are Looking beyond Ghetto Violence." *New York Times,* 11 September: B1.

Williams, Linda. 1987. "'Something Else besides a Mother': Stella Dallas and the Maternal Melodrama." *Home Is Where the Heart Is: Studies in Melodrama and the Woman's Film,* ed. Christine Gledhill, 229–325. London: British Film Institute.

INDEX